A GRIM ALMANAC OF
BIRMINGHAM

A GRIM ALMANAC OF
BIRMINGHAM

KAREN EVANS

First published 2015

The History Press
The Mill, Brimscombe Port
Stroud, Gloucestershire, GL5 2QG
www.thehistorypress.co.uk

British Library Cataloguing in Publication Data.
A catalogue record for this book is available from the British Library.

ISBN 978 0 7509 5960 5

Typesetting and origination by The History Press
Printed in Great Britain

CONTENTS

INTRODUCTION & ACKNOWLEDGEMENTS

All of the grim events mentioned in this book are from contemporary newspaper accounts. Many of the stories differed greatly from one newspaper to the next, especially the spellings of names, so the records of these dark deeds are only as accurate as the accounts I have used. When I began my research, I couldn't believe that people could treat one another with such violence and disregard for life. I was also shocked at how many children died in fire-related incidents – I think there could have been an event for this tragedy every day of the year.

I would like to thank the following people for their contributions of information, illustrations and advice: Dennis Neale (www.blackcountrymuse.com); Ian Gibb; Lee Fellows; M. Smith; Will Knowles; and Ken, Pat and Ian Upton. Thank you also to The History Press, and particularly my commissioning editor Matilda Richards, for all her help and encouragement. I must send my love to Pete, Imogen and Pierce for their unstinting patience again! And finally, to all my colleagues at Delves Junior for making me feel so special.

Every effort has been made to clear copyright; however, my apologies to anyone I might have inadvertently missed. I can assure you it was not deliberate but an oversight on my part.

I would like to dedicate this book to my beloved and much missed grandparents who had their own fantastic stories to tell.

Karen Evans, 2015

JANUARY

1 JANUARY 1893 Sixty-five-year-old coach painter William Bolas had recently returned to his home in Macdonald Street after losing his sight. Bolas seemed depressed and, on 29 December 1892, asked a friend named James Cartwright to buy a razor so he could shave. Cartwright refused, however, believing Bolas wished to harm himself. On the morning of 30 December, Bolas' landlady found him in his room in agony and realised that he had swallowed his wooden walking stick, a piece of which could still be seen sticking up at the back of his throat. The landlady's son attempted to pull out the stick but the sudden pain caused Bolas to bite his finger. A constable was called and successfully extracted about 16in of cane. This caused Bolas to vomit violently and another piece of wood, approximately 15in in length, was pulled from his mouth. He was taken to the workhouse infirmary but died on this day from serious injuries to his windpipe. The inquest, three days later, returned a verdict of suicide whilst temporarily insane.

2 JANUARY 1892 A group of friends, including nineteen-year-old screw maker Walter Eaves and twenty-year-old William Edward Russell, met up at the Stores beerhouse, Bristol Street, on this Saturday evening. The men decided to challenge each other by trying to see who could withstand the hardest blow to the chest. Eaves punched Russell, who then returned the blow. They agreed to try again but this time Russell collapsed unconscious to the floor and died almost immediately. Eaves was arrested on charges of manslaughter and tried at Birmingham Assizes in March. The post-mortem revealed heart failure as a result of the blow but, as there was no question the men thought the activity was dangerous, Eaves was acquitted.

3 JANUARY 1836 When sixteen-month-old Mary Maullin showed signs of a bad cold this Sunday, her carpenter father decided to dose her with a 'Morrison Pill', which he swore by to cure any ills. With the help of his wife and neighbours at Sandpits, the pills were ground down, mixed with water and fed to the child. Little Mary showed no real sign of improvement, however, and over the next few days, her father fed her several more pills, including the more purgative 'No. 2 Pill', used to open the bowels. By Wednesday evening, Mary seemed in acute distress and the family finally called in a doctor who ordered leeches. Sadly the little girl died on Thursday evening in considerable pain. A post-mortem revealed twenty large patches of bleeding ulcerations in her intestines, caused by gamboge in the pills she had ingested. At the inquest, Mary's father admitted giving his daughter up to fourteen pills a day but explained that she had been taking them since birth and 'a nice fat baby it was'. The coroner, in summing up, did not blame the parents but felt that the public's perception of the use of 'Morrison Pills' was ill judged and that Mary had died from their incautious usage.

4 JANUARY 1873 After spending this evening at a local public house, thirty-one-year-old hawker Eli Williams was making his way home to Blews Terrace, George Street West, when he met his neighbour, thirty-year-old marble polisher John Lyndon, who was also rather the worse for wear. The two men were not on friendly terms and Lyndon struck Williams a blow to the face, telling him that he had been waiting a week to do so. Williams quickly retaliated and the men began to fight in earnest before Williams felled Lyndon with a blow to the side of the head. Lyndon collapsed into the crowd of spectators and died moments later. Williams was arrested on a charge of manslaughter but the judge at Birmingham Assizes in March 1873 discharged him, ruling that he had merely acted in self-defence.

5 JANUARY 1883 When thirty-year-old Mary Ann Shelswell intervened in the argument between John Cooke and his wife on this Saturday evening, she could have had no idea of the consequences of her actions. Twenty-seven-year-old John Cooke, a hawker from Devon Street, Vauxhall, had been drinking heavily and followed Shelswell back to her home in Saltley Road where he found her talking to a neighbour. Without another word he swung a chopper he was carrying and struck her in the head, causing a wound over 1in long and resulting in a compound fracture to her skull. As she fell to the floor, Cooke continued to beat her with his fists even though she was unconscious. Shelswell was rushed to the General Hospital while Cooke was arrested. She survived the ordeal and Cooke was brought before Birmingham Quarter Sessions to be charged with malicious wounding. Found guilty, he was sentenced to five years' penal servitude.

6 JANUARY 1882 Lauretta Frances Salt worked as a 'wrapper-uper' at the warehouse of Messrs Empson and Harding in Oxford Street, Stirchley. The nineteen year old, who lived with her parents in Edward Street, was in the warehouse with other workers this Friday afternoon when the floor suddenly gave way, precipitating Salt and two others into the room below. Salt was buried beneath at least 7cwt of debris, including a box containing a quantity of tin. It took some twenty minutes to uncover her body and the post-mortem revealed that the girl had suffocated due to the pressure on her chest. The building was declared not fit for purpose and a verdict of accidental death was passed.

7 JANUARY 1842 Although they had been married for less than two years, thirty-year-old painter Ezra Steapenhill and his twenty-six-year-old wife Bassillissa of Heneage Street, Aston, already had a reputation as an unhappy couple. On this

Friday evening, Ezra was cleaning a shotgun in the sitting room, laying it on a table by the fire while Bassillissa played with their young daughter on a nearby chair. Suddenly and without warning, the gun went off. The shot hit Bassillissa in the chest and she fell to the floor, fatally injured with internal injuries to her heart, lungs and liver; she was dead before the doctor could arrive. The gun was examined and found to have a faulty lock, but the post-mortem, together with the couple's unhappy relationship, led to Ezra's arrest. The post-mortem had indicated that the gun must have been raised diagonally not horizontally when it discharged and Ezra was accused of the wilful murder of his wife. He stood trial at the Warwick Assizes in March 1842 but the jury felt that there was insufficient evidence to prove Ezra had intended to kill his wife and he was released without charge.

8 JANUARY 1889 On this day, George Nicholson was hanged at Warwick Gaol for the murder of Mary Ann Eccleston. When fifty-two-year-old master baker George married fifty-three-year-old widow Mary Ann in 1883, he had a successful business in Birmingham. However, in 1885 the bakery failed because of George's drinking and the family were forced to move to Burlington Street, Aston. From then on, George could only find irregular work as a journeyman baker and the couple frequently argued about money, particularly as Mary Ann and her children were providing most of the income to keep the home together. On the evening of 22 September, neighbours heard the pair quarrelling; then there was silence, followed by the sounds of someone leaving the house. About an hour later, Albert James Eccleston, Mary Ann's son, came home and walked into the sitting room to find a scene of horror. His mother was sitting in a rocking chair by the fire, her skull battered in five places and her brain protruding. There was blood all over the floor and a hatchet was discovered in the corner of the room, wet with blood and with some of Mary Ann's hair stuck to the blade. Mary Ann was still alive but died before help arrived. George, meanwhile, was spotted pawning his wife's watch in Birmingham before being arrested in Walsall. He strenuously denied any involvement in Mary Ann's death, although his clothes showed signs of blood. At the Warwick Assizes on 17 December, George's defence argued that it was a case of manslaughter but the jury found him guilty of murder and sentenced him to death.

9 JANUARY 1877 At the Birmingham Police Court on this day, twenty-three-year-old bricklayer William Naughton of Lower Brearley Street was charged with violently assaulting his wife, Ann, on the previous evening. It appeared that Naughton had come home extremely drunk and began to beat her in a brutal manner. Ann escaped from the house but Naughton followed her, knocking her down and kicking her in the face and shoulders until she lost consciousness. In his defence, Naughton told the court that he had returned home to find no fire in the grate and his wife drunk in a nearby public house. The court found him guilty and sentenced Naughton to six weeks' imprisonment.

10 JANUARY 1891 Twenty-six-year-old nail maker George Gallagher of New Canal Street had been seeing his paramour Kate Callighan only a short time when he demanded that she become a streetwalker to support him. When, on this Saturday evening, she refused, Gallagher struck her several times and kicked her so hard in the face that he split her lip right through. Tried at Birmingham Police Court on 13 January, the Bench found Gallagher guilty of assault and sent him to prison for two months' hard labour.

11 JANUARY 1895 This day saw the inquest into the death of thirty-five-year-old ironworker Edward Birch of Upper Highgate Street. When Edward married Selina Jones, she already had a daughter called Caroline. Over the years, Edward and Caroline, who was nicknamed Carrie, became increasingly close, with some questioning if the relationship was really that of father and daughter. Edward was particularly angry when Carrie, now eighteen years old, was seen with other men and, in 1894, he wrote a letter accusing her of immoral behaviour. On the afternoon of 7 January, Edward told his wife that he was working late, while that same evening Carrie went out saying she was going to evening school. At about eleven o'clock, police were attracted by groans coming from a field in Sparkbrook. They found Carrie stabbed to death and Birch barely alive, with his throat cut and a strong smell of carbolic acid. Edward was taken to the Queen's Hospital but died early the next morning. Police soon suspected that Edward was responsible for both Carrie's death and his own – Carrie's body was laid out in the field and there were traces of carbolic acid in her throat – so when letters were found where

Edward told his parents he was going to die, they were unsurprised. There was some indication that it was a suicide pact but the inquest jury returned a verdict of murder on the body of Caroline Jones and recorded that Edward had committed suicide. The undertaker decided to raise money for the widow and the remaining six children by charging the public 1d to see the bodies of the couple; this continued until the police intervened.

12 JANUARY 1884 Charles Amos Elkington, a forty-eight-year-old stoker from Clarke Street, Ladywood, had only been working at Messrs Thomas Bolton & Sons' metal works in Broad Street for five weeks. At about nine o'clock this Saturday morning, Elkington was in the boiler house, firing the flue of a Cornish boiler that had not been used for several weeks, when the flue suddenly collapsed, tearing the metal plates and allowing the steam to escape from the boiler. Elkington was enveloped in the steam and badly scalded. Although he was quickly taken to the Queen's Hospital, he succumbed to his injuries later that day. The inquest heard that the exploded boiler had not been serviced in three years so, although the jury returned a verdict of accidental death on the married father of three, they recommended that Messrs Bolton have their boilers properly inspected.

13 JANUARY 1896 On this Monday morning, sixty-one-year-old boiler maker John Taylor of Norman Street, Winson Green, was working at Messrs Tangyes when a heavy boilerplate, which was leaning against a wall, suddenly tipped forward and fell on him. The metal fractured the base of John's skull and crushed one of his legs so severely that it was almost severed from his body. The married father of four was taken to the General Hospital but he died of his injuries at three o'clock this afternoon.

14 JANUARY 1861 A group of platelayers and a railway inspector were working in the New Street south tunnel at about eleven o'clock this Monday night when a worker called out to say that a train was coming in. Forty-seven-year-old inspector Thomas Dilks and platelayer William Bonham stepped on to the up line but, in the darkness, they did not see a set of carriages being shunted along. The carriages knocked Dilks, a married father of eleven, under the wheels where he was crushed and killed instantly. Bonham was caught on the side of his body, fracturing his right arm and smashing the side of his face; he was taken to the General Hospital, where his arm was amputated. Sadly, Bonham's injuries proved serious and he died five days later. Although evidence suggested that the shunting engine did not blow a warning whistle, the inquests returned verdicts of accidental deaths on the two men.

15 JANUARY 1858 Towards the end of October 1857, Emma Smith gave birth to her illegitimate son in the workhouse. From the moment of George William's birth, Emma refused to care for him properly saying, 'If it were not for you, you little d___, I might go and have a home at my mothers ... you will keep me in the workhouse all my life.' The baby was often left in a filthy condition and Emma regularly had to be forced to feed him at the breast or give him food. Witnesses saw Emma adding salt to his pap so he was sick and pinching his tiny body. In the middle of December 1857, George contracted bronchitis, which the workhouse surgeon felt was not serious. However, after initially responding well, the little boy suddenly became extremely unwell, dying on 3 January. An inquest took place on this day and the post-mortem revealed that the baby was suffering from a severe want of nourishment. It could not be determined if the death had proceeded from emaciation, however, and as a result the jury returned a verdict of death by visitation of God but wished to convey their detestation of Emma's conduct.

16 JANUARY 1877 After her husband's death, thirty-year-old Mary Saunders began living with her paramour Frederick Edwin Baker, a thirty-year-old barman, in Lichfield Road, Aston. Frederick wanted to marry Mary but she obviously didn't feel the same way and would frequently be seen around the area in the company of other men. Baker became increasing jealous, particularly when Mary seemed to favour George Silvers, a former friend of her late husband. On Monday, 15 January, Mary and George spent the evening together before returning to Lichfield Road where Frederick refused to allow Silvers into the house and began violently arguing with Mary. Neighbours reported hearing shouting until two o'clock the following morning before all became quiet. At approximately nine o'clock on the morning of Tuesday, 16 January, a servant living at Lichfield Road came downstairs and, in the semi-darkness, stepped on Mary's body. Mary's throat had been cut from ear to ear, so deeply that she was almost decapitated. The police were summoned but Baker had gone. Tracked down in Stafford two days later, he made no attempt to deny killing Mary but claimed she had been playing him false with other men, including Silvers. At the inquest, Frederick saw Silvers in court and became extremely agitated, threatening to kill him: 'Oh let me have him for five minutes and then hang me. Take my neck and have done with it.' Unsurprisingly, Baker was tried and found guilty at Warwick Assizes on 20 March. Executed at Warwick Gaol by hangman William Marwood on 17 April, Baker admitted the justice of his sentence and hoped that his fate would be a warning to others.

WILLIAM MARWOOD, FROM THE WAX MODEL IN MADAME TUSSAUD'S.

William Marwood, executioner.

17 JANUARY 1891 The continuing cold weather meant that Park Mills Pool, private water in Nechells, was frozen over. On the afternoon of 16 January this proved too much temptation for a group of boys, including ten-year-old Charles Ernest Acton, who climbed through a gap in the fence to play on the ice. Acton, who lived on Cheatham Street, was sliding across the frozen pool when a crack suddenly appeared and he fell backwards into a hole, disappearing beneath the ice. Friends and witnesses tried to rescue the boy but more cracks appeared and the body wasn't retrieved until early this Saturday morning when police used a boat to drag the pool. Acton was found with his feet embedded in the mud bottom. The inquest returned a verdict of accidental death after recommending that police should be paid to attend private pools.

18 JANUARY 1841 In early 1841, seventeen-year-old farm servant Thomas Nicholas purchased a large horse pistol to shoot birds and, on this Sunday morning, was on his way to some fields near Minworth when he saw Thomas Fellows. Fearing he might be questioned about the pistol, Nicholas rammed it into his trouser pocket, muzzle upwards, so that it wouldn't be seen. However, just after passing Fellows the pistol went off, causing a wound 4in in length and exposing the bone and nerves. Fellows ran back to the heavily bleeding Nicholas and led him to a nearby house where he was conveyed to the Birmingham hospital. Unfortunately, the wound proved too great and Thomas Nicholas died from his injuries three days later; the subsequent inquest returned a verdict of accidental death.

19 JANUARY 1865 Sixteen-year-old John James of Communication Row worked as a soda water maker for a soda water manufactory in Broad Street. On this Thursday afternoon, James was playing with a piece of string in the bottling department, throwing it at a rapidly revolving shaft and then unwrapping it. His game went horribly wrong, however, when the string caught around his left hand. James was drawn up by the spinning shaft and thrown around several times before the machinery was turned off and he landed on some empty crates. He was taken to the Queen's Hospital suffering from broken ribs and severe cuts but, after initially making good progress, he contracted tetanus and died on 2 February. A verdict of accidental death was returned on the unfortunate youth.

20 JANUARY 1877 When thirty-five-year-old Susannah Norbury answered the door of her house in Ryland Road, Edgbaston, late on this Saturday evening, she was shocked to see her twenty-seven-year-old neighbour Jane Powell covered in blood and asking for help. It soon transpired that the blood was from Powell's

forty-seven-year-old husband Thomas, who was lying severely injured in his kitchen with a large, 6in-deep stab wound in his abdomen. Jane maintained that Thomas had stabbed himself but asked Susannah to help hide her bloody apron and carving knife. Thomas was taken to Queen's Hospital but he died a few hours later and suspicion fell on Jane, who was arrested for murder and Susannah for an accessory after the fact. The Birmingham Stipendiary decided that the evidence against Susannah was inconclusive and discharged her but Jane was committed for trial at Warwick Assizes on 27 March. The prosecution argued Jane had killed her husband during a drunken quarrel but the jury felt there was no direct proof and she was acquitted.

21 JANUARY 1868 After breaking her leg in the winter of 1867, Miss Mary Milbourne needed someone to do odd jobs around the house. Mary's cousin, Mrs Beasley, assisted the sixty-one year old for some weeks and it was during this time that she realised Mary kept several hundred pounds in the house. Mrs Beasley discussed this with her stepsons – Thomas Beasley, a costermonger; Joseph Beasley, a twenty-one-year-old shoemaker; and William Beasley, a twenty-seven-year-old costermonger – and they came up with a plan to steal the money. Along with thirty-five-year-old hawker Charles Grayson and his wife Elizabeth, the brothers went to Miss Milbourne's home in Heneage Street on this Tuesday afternoon and, believing the house to be empty all day, broke a window in the kitchen to gain access. However, as the gang searched for the money, Mary returned and, realising she was being burgled, she tried to call for help. In a frantic effort to avoid detection, a member of the group grabbed Mary by the throat and suffocated her. Unable to find the stash of money, the thieves fled with only a few pounds, which they split between themselves, and Thomas went to Bristol. Miss Milbourne's body was soon discovered and, when a £50 reward was offered, a witness called John Mack came forward to tell the police he had been with the Beasley brothers when they were discussing the break-in. The Beasleys and Graysons were arrested. Thomas Beasley admitted stealing from the house but said none of the others had entered the building and a man named George had killed Mary. At Warwick Assizes in March 1868, Mack's evidence was shaken in cross-examination while several of the prisoners had an alibi. Thomas was sentenced to fourteen years' imprisonment for robbery but the others were found not guilty and discharged. 'George' was never traced.

22 JANUARY 1859 On 20 January 1859, fifty-year-old widow Sarah Brane and her daughter were at New Street Station meeting a relative who was arriving at four o'clock. Sarah decided to pop back to her house in Gooch Street and was attempting to cross the line near the Queen Street entrance when an engine suddenly

came up the line. Railway policeman Joseph Pass realised the danger and attempted to push Mrs Brane out of danger. Unfortunately, the buffer of the tender caught her and knocked her under the train. When the train passed it was clear Sarah was dead; her skulled had been fractured and the engine wheels had amputated her foot. The inquest today returned a verdict of accidental death.

23 JANUARY 1894 Thirty-six-year-old Henry William Gill of Wastwater, Yardley Road, Acock's Green was a partner in the firm of Ash, Gill & Co. electricians, Bletchworth Works, Birmingham. He had recently patented a new electrical process, which was being acquired by a London syndicate, and the future was looking extremely prosperous. On this Tuesday evening, Gill remained in the office alone to write some letters and at some point decided to drink some whiskey. Needing some water for the alcohol, Gill went into one of the rooms and poured what he believed was water from a jug. Tragically, the liquid was actually cyanide of potassium and Gill fell to the floor in agony. When workers arrived the next morning, they found Gill dead with the jug close by. The inquest jury returned a verdict of death by misadventure and the coroner remarked that it was an extraordinary thing that such a poison should not be kept under lock and key. Gill left a pregnant widow and three young children.

24 JANUARY 1891 Five-month-old William Edward Parrott lived with his parents Henry and Sarah Parrott and his four siblings in appalling conditions at No. 23 Court, No. 5 House, Lower Tower Street. Eighteen months ago, bailiffs had taken away various pieces of furniture, including a bed, leaving the family of seven just one bed to sleep in. On this Saturday night, Henry (who was drunk), Emma and the five children retired to bed but woke in the night to find baby William had been overlain and suffocated. At the inquest the deputy coroner said that the death was evidently due to overcrowding but he did not know what could be done; the jury returned a verdict of accidental death and thought the father was deserving of censure for not providing for his children.

25 JANUARY 1894 On this Thursday morning, seven-year-old Rose Collins went to several neighbours near her home at No. 7 Court, No. 9 House, New Summer Street, asking for urgent assistance. When they arrived at the Collins' home they found forty-year-old Catherine Collins cradling her unconscious ten-year-old son, Robert, who was bleeding heavily from a head wound. The neighbours tried to staunch the blood and took Robert to the General Hospital but he died soon after. Robert was found to have a circular punctured wound to the scalp, which penetrated through the skull into his brain. When questioned, Catherine gave several versions of the circumstances that led to the injury but finally admitted that she had thrown a poker at Robert because he was misbehaving. The poker caught Robert in the head but he seemed fine when the poker was removed; however, he suddenly collapsed ten minutes later. Catherine pleaded guilty to manslaughter at Birmingham Assizes and was sentenced to two months' imprisonment with hard labour.

26 JANUARY 1860 On 11 December 1859, Mary Heeley was in the yard of her home in Carey's Court, Moor Street, when eighteen-year-old James Davitt (accompanied by his brother Thomas and Edward Finn) approached her using 'indecent language'. When she ignored him, he grabbed at her throat and tried to strike her. Luckily, at that moment her father, Martin, and brother, John, appeared. John Heeley intervened but Thomas Davitt suddenly produced a hammer, striking Martin Heeley so hard that his skull suffered a compound fracture from the blow. John went to his father's aid but was attacked by Thomas, James and Finn so severely that he was left unconscious on the floor. The two Heeleys were taken to the General Hospital where Martin's life was despaired of for a while. Over the next few weeks their three attackers were arrested and this day saw them brought before Birmingham Police Court on the charge of assault. The magistrate considered the evidence against James and Finn insufficient but Thomas Davitt was committed for trial. At Birmingham Quarter Sessions in April 1860, Thomas was found guilty of malicious wounding and sentenced to eighteen months' imprisonment.

27 JANUARY 1883 This day saw an inquest into the death of twelve-year-old Mary Elizabeth Hassam of Wharf Street. Mary's mother Emma told the coroner that the family of eight occupied only two bedrooms and Mary (the only daughter) slept in her parents' room with three other siblings. On Monday, 22 January, Mary showed signs of a severe cold. Emma tried to treat it with cough medicine and moved the girl into the smaller bedroom, which had no fireplace. Mr Barratt, a surgeon, was called and recommended moving Mary into the downstairs parlour in front of the fire. Unfortunately, Mary was suffering from an inflammation of the lungs that quickly turned into pneumonia and, despite every attention, she died on the Wednesday evening. Mr Barratt ascribed Mary's death to her atrocious living conditions and felt that the whole court was unfit for human inhabitation; the coroner sympathised with Emma in trying to treat the girl 'in that wretched place, which the authorities allowed to be let to poor people' and the jury returned a verdict of death from natural causes.

28 **JANUARY** 1837 At about six o'clock this Saturday evening, midwife Rebecca Tong was called to the home of Henry and Ann White in Vauxhall Road to assist in the birth of their child. Although the labour was easy the baby boy was stillborn. Mr White, when called to the room, was intoxicated and belligerent, exclaiming, 'you have brought me up to see a b__y dead thing' before leaving. Neighbours, who had aided Ann, told the midwife that Henry had treated his wife very roughly, including sitting on her stomach and threatening to cut off the baby's head when it was born. When Rebecca called a few days later, Ann was bruised on her face and the midwife saw Mr White strike his wife saying, 'die you b___r'. By 1 February, Ann's health had deteriorated to such an extent that she was removed to the workhouse infirmary where it became clear she was bleeding excessively after the birth. Although she rallied for a while, Ann died on 4 February. An inquest revealed Henry's violent and drunken behaviour in the weeks leading up to the birth and described how he had thrown his full weight on to his wife hours after the delivery, placed his hands around her neck and told her that he hoped she would die. However, as there were no marks of violence on the baby and the surgeon attributed Ann's death to 'flooding', the inquest jury decided that they had both died natural deaths and Henry White was released without charge.

29 **JANUARY** 1872 When thirty-two-year-old labourer Henry Boden began lodging with eighty-year-old Mary Sanders at her home in Sherborne Street, he started paying his addresses to her twenty-five-year-old niece Mary Ann Jones. On the evening of 27 January, Boden came home drunk and, when the women complained, he remarked that 'he was in no mood to be played with'. When Jones continued to rebuke him, Henry pushed her off the chair so she banged her face on a nearby table. Sanders, who was in the yard hanging clothes on the line, felt a 'stunning' sensation on the back of her head before she lost consciousness; Boden had hit the old woman with a poker. Henry then returned to Jones and struck her several times before she managed to escape and call for assistance for herself and her aunt, who was taken to Queen's Hospital. Charged with two counts of assault at Birmingham Police Court on this day, Boden apologised for his behaviour, blaming jealousy; the magistrate told Henry he should consider himself fortunate that he was not standing in the dock charged with murder, before sentencing him to twelve months' imprisonment with hard labour.

30 **JANUARY** 1837 As twenty-seven-year-old labourer John Roberts was on his way home this Monday evening, he met two men in Witton Road who he recognised as railroad labourers. One of the men, seeing Roberts, said 'D__n his eyes, knock him into the ditch' at which the other, Edward David Nicks, ran at Roberts, knocked him

down and kneed him in the stomach. Luckily for Roberts, several witnesses came to his assistance and he was able to break free without further injury. Although one man escaped, Nicks was taken into custody and brought before Birmingham Police Court on 2 February, charged with assault. Nicks said he remembered nothing as he had been drunk at the time but the Bench, after commenting upon the impossibility of anyone being able to pass safely through Witton or Aston owing to the violence of the railway employees, found him guilty and fined him 5s.

31 JANUARY 1890 This day saw the inquest concerning the death of fifteen-year-old George Smith of Adderley at the paper works of Messrs Smith, Stone and Knight on Landoe Street. On 16 January 1890, Smith finished work for the day and went to the boiler house to ask permission to leave. A steam-run grindstone was working in the room when the stone, weighing about 17cwt, suddenly split and pieces flew across the boiler house. Smith was hit in the back of the head, thrown to the floor and began bleeding profusely from the mouth and nose. He was rushed to the General Hospital where he was diagnosed with a severely fractured skull but he died shortly after. At the inquest it was found that the spindle hole in the grindstone was too small and the engine had been spinning at a velocity of about 200 revolutions a minute, which was considered in excess of a speed consistent with safety. The jury returned a verdict of accidental death but suggested precaution should be made to regulate the speed at which grindstones were worked.

FEBRUARY

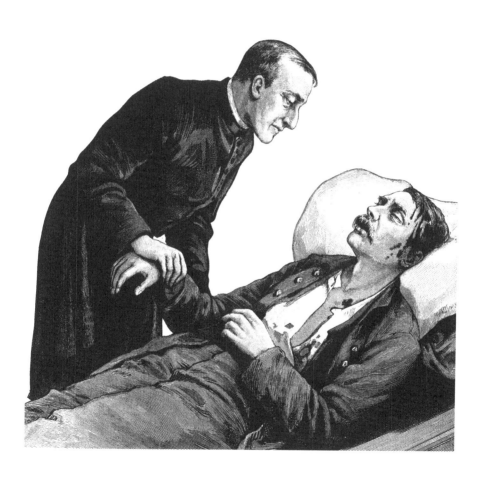

1   FEBRUARY 1846 When an unknown man collapsed in the street on this Sunday morning, he was taken first to the police station and then to the workhouse where he died a few hours later. Evidence on the body and statements from witnesses seemed to identify the man as forty-two-year-old William Sumner and he was buried as such. However, five weeks later, a William Wall from Derby arrived in the city claiming that the body was of his father, Thomas Wall, who had been missing since 16 February. Despite the obvious disparity in dates, the body was exhumed and examined by William Wall and his mother who swore that the decaying corpse was Thomas. Surgeons pointed out that the marks on the neck and legs, which the family took for scars, were in fact decomposition and a former employer of Wall said the body was too tall to be the missing man. The inquiry decided that the body was William Sumner and reburied him; Thomas Wall was never found.

2   FEBRUARY 1865 When bricklayer John Bateman married Susan she already had an illegitimate son, also called John. John Bateman Senior adopted John Junior and the family lived together in Moor Street. However, as John Junior grew older, he was often violent to his parents and on one occasion he stabbed his stepfather with a bayonet, kicked him in the stomach and blackened his eyes. At about one o'clock on 1 January 1865, twenty-five-year-old John Junior returned home intoxicated and began quarrelling with his stepfather, pulling out a knife in an attempt to stab him. Fifty-two-year-old John Senior, fearing for his life, grabbed a pair of iron tongs and hit the younger man over the head, causing a wound 3in in length and 1in in breadth. John Junior collapsed and was rushed to the General Hospital where his brain became inflamed and he died today. John Bateman was tried for manslaughter at Warwick Assizes on 2 March but the jury felt that he had clearly acted in self-defence and he was acquitted.

3   FEBRUARY 1881 Single woman Sophia Mellor had managed to procure lodging with her four-year-old daughter Ada at the house of fifty-seven-year-old brass founder John Mills and his family in Ashted Row. On this Thursday morning, Sophia left for work, leaving Ada in the kitchen, with Mr Mills and one of his sons in another part of the house. During the morning, according to Mill's son, Ada shouted out so John went into the kitchen in a great rage, coming out a few minutes later and telling his son that Ada was dirty so he had poured the kettle water on her. When Mrs Mills came home she found Ada in great distress with a large burn or scald on her back some 5in in diameter. Mrs Mills told Sophia she would take Ada to the General Hospital but, when nothing was done to this effect,

Sophia took the child herself. The wound was so deep that bone was clearly visible and the horrified doctor admitted Ada straight away. Ada, too terrified to explain how she was injured, died on 7 March from pneumonia brought on by the scalding. At the inquest on 11 March, John Mills was found guilty of manslaughter and sent to Warwick Assizes but the assize jury decided that Mills was unaware of the true temperature of the water and found him not guilty.

4 FEBRUARY 1868 Unable to fend for herself and her daughter, sixty-year-old Mary Pritchett entered Erdington Workhouse with twenty-three-year-old Mary Ann Pritchett early in February. Within a few days the two women and another inmate named Mary Baker were found to be suffering from the 'itch' so were moved to a separate ward where they were prescribed a lotion of sulphur and lime. However, on this Tuesday evening, in the absence of the regular nurse, her assistant Louisa Bosworth went to the surgery and picked up a bottle of carbolic acid by mistake. Bosworth smeared the three women with this lotion but when they were all seized with dreadful pains she called for help and the dreadful truth was uncovered. Medical aid was given but although Mary Baker recovered, Mrs Pritchett died a few hours later and, after lingering in great pain, Mary Ann died on 6 February. The inquest returned a verdict of accidental death but censured the workhouse board for not employing sufficient nurses.

5 FEBRUARY 1858 On 29 January 1858, thirty-three-year-old draper Ebenezer John Harrison arrived at the Clarendon Hotel, Upper Temple Street with Ann Chapman who was calling herself Ebenezer's wife. According to the hotel staff the couple seemed to have 'lived temperately and frequently went out' but paid bills promptly. On this Friday morning, Ann was lying in bed when Ebenezer revealed a pair of pistols saying, 'Ann, I intend one of these for you and the other for myself.' Ann jumped up but Ebenezer assured her they were not loaded and encouraged her to lie on the bed. A few minutes later, he suddenly grabbed Ann's hair and fired the pistol in her ear. Stunned, bleeding and in considerable pain, with a fractured right temple bone, Ann rushed out of the room while hotel staff came to her assistance. They found Ebenezer lying dead across the bed, a bullet hole through the roof of his mouth. At the inquest Ann was able to testify to Ebenezer's suspicious nature and a letter written by the dead man was found in the hotel room, revealing his state of mind: 'My only reason for doing as I have done is I am jealous of her ... she has not been honest to me ... and I have made up my mind if I cannot have her no one else shall.' The inquest returned a verdict of death by concussion of the spine caused by a pistol shot, fired while in a state of insanity.

6   FEBRUARY 1892   Just before midnight on this Saturday night, the Russian Von Wilski was sitting with his friends at the George Inn, Inge Street, when a gang of youths broke down the door. Von was hit over the head with a bottle by one of the men before the others assaulted him with belts. Von did not recognise any of his attackers and knew of no motive for the assault. The police were called and, seeing twenty-year-old John Newport in the street, Von informed the officer that 'he was one of them'. Newport of Warwick Street denied any involvement but was arrested nevertheless. This seemed to have ignited the ire of several youths who blamed the local Jewish community for Newport's arrest and they assaulted a German Jew named David Fiddler the next morning. Birmingham Police Court sentenced the ruffians to between one month and two months' imprisonment with hard labour for the racially motivated attacks.

7   FEBRUARY 1882   Joseph William Pearmain was employed as a stableman by Mr Hunt of Hagley Road. On the evening of 6 February, thirty-nine-year-old Pearmain of Sherlock Street returned to the stables after a day's hunting and, rather the worse for drink, began taunting thirty-two-year-old George Davis. When Pearmain told Davis he was 'more of a gardener' than a stableman, Davis took offence and the two men started to argue in earnest. Pearmain went to hit Davis but Davis had a straw fork in his hand and struck Pearmain across the head with the wooden handle. Pearmain reeled backwards, hitting his head against an iron stall post but he soon recovered and hit Davis across the face. Davis punched Pearmain who fell unconscious to the floor. After about an hour, Pearmain regained consciousness and went to the Hen and Chickens public house in New Street for a drink. However, later that evening Pearmain was found insensible and taken to the General Hospital, where he died early on this Tuesday morning. Davis was arrested on a charge of manslaughter and stood trial at Warwick Assizes on 5 August 1882. However, the post-mortem revealed that Pearmain had died from a skull fracture and bleeding on the brain caused by hitting his head on the post so Davis was acquitted.

8 FEBRUARY 1878 Twenty-three-year-old Thomas Evans of Wednesbury was employed at Messrs Payton's tube works in Smethwick. On this Friday evening, Evans was by the wicket gate of Handsworth railway station waiting to catch the train home when he heard an engine approaching. Evans shouted to his friends, 'The train is coming and I shall not have time to get a ticket' while running towards the platform but it is believed he stumbled and fell on to the tracks. The engine cut poor Evans to pieces; at Swan Village the driver found the unfortunate man's foot and part of his leg caught between the wheels. The inquest, held three days later, returned a verdict of accidental death.

9 FEBRUARY 1894 When their mother died in October 1893, eleven-year-old Alice Beatrice Poole and nine-year-old Violet Maud Poole were handed over to the care of Elizabeth Greatrex who lived in No. 12, back of No. 126, Hospital Street. Their lives before Mrs Poole's death had not been pleasant, as their father Samuel was a heavy drinker and neglectful, but the girls' situation was to deteriorate even further. When an inspector from the Birmingham Society for the Prevention of Cruelty to Children visited Violet and Alice in January 1894, he found them dressed in dirty rags and covered in vermin, with clothing given to them at school having been pawned by Mrs Greatrex to buy drink. The girls told the inspector that they sold firewood every day until eleven o'clock at night and if they were out in the rain they had to go to bed in their wet clothes. The beds were sacks on the floor with an old coat to cover them and the Poole girls were inadequately fed. Brought before Birmingham Police Court on this day, Mrs Greatrex complained that Samuel gave her no money to look after his daughters and was not interested in their welfare. Samuel Poole and Elizabeth were found guilty of wantonly neglecting the children and causing them bodily suffering; Poole was sentenced to two months' imprisonment and Greatrex one month's hard labour. Alice and Violet were removed to the society's care.

10 FEBRUARY 1881 At Birmingham Police Court on this day, twenty-eight-year-old brass founder Edward Jacques of Hockley was summoned for assaulting his wife Mary Ann on 5 February. Mary Ann, who appeared in court with two black eyes, told magistrates that although she had married Edward three years before, they had not lived together for over six months due to his violent and abusive behaviour. On the day in question, the couple met by accident and Edward became verbally aggressive before striking Mary Ann in the face several times. Edward told the court that his wife had been violent first but the father of one was found guilty

of assault and sentenced to one month's imprisonment and bound over to keep the peace for six months.

11 **FEBRUARY** 1869 Fifty-five-year-old Thomas Phillips of Snow's Buildings, Cregoe Street, worked as an iron caster at the Britannia Foundry in Bradford Street. On this Thursday afternoon, Phillips was in the casting shop filling moulds with molten iron in ladles when he failed to lift his ladle high enough. The bottom struck the mould and tipped the liquid metal on to the floor and into Phillips' left boot. His fellow workers quickly removed the boot and took him to the General Hospital where his foot was dressed but, by 3 March, it was clear that the lower part of his leg was damaged beyond repair and it was amputated. After the amputation, Phillips became delirious, dying of congestion of the lungs on 3 April. The jury returned a verdict of accidental death on the married father of five.

12 **FEBRUARY** 1840 This evening saw a verdict of accidental death at the inquest of gardener Thomas Hands. On 11 February, Hands was engaged in cropping some trees in the garden of Mr Proud of Edgbaston. It appears he was standing on one of the branches severing another and, when it was nearly cut, shifted along the branch to avoid falling debris. Unfortunately, on this occasion Hands did not get out of the way quickly enough. The end of the branch struck him on the head and he fell senseless to the ground. Fellow workmen took Mr Hands to his home in Tennant Street but he never regained consciousness, dying on this day of his injuries.

13 **FEBRUARY** 1864 After finishing work at seven o'clock on the evening of 11 February, fourteen-year-old George Shipton was in his parents' room at No. 36 Communication Row when he noticed a brandy bottle on the mantelpiece. He took a drink and then left the house. At nine o'clock his sister Sarah Ann met him on the canal bridge in Bath Row where George appeared to be intoxicated and she demanded what was the matter. George explained he had drunk some of their father's brandy and 'that had made me tipsy'. The brother and sister went home and it was then realised the brandy bottle actually contained liniment for gout which included belladonna and aconite. A doctor was sent for but George lapsed into unconsciousness and died within the hour. The inquest held on this day found that every precaution had been taken with the medicine, as it had not been within easy reach and the label was overwritten with the word 'poison', so a verdict of accidental death was returned.

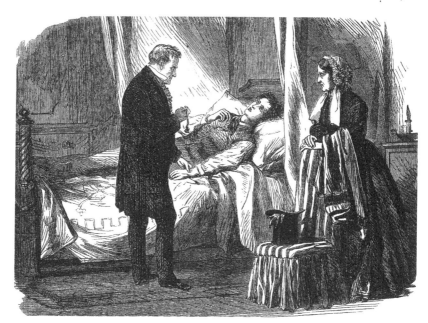

14 FEBRUARY 1871 Fourteen-year-old George Smith of Lilly Green, Derby Street, worked on the boring machine at Messrs Blews & Sons, Bartholomew Street. On this Tuesday morning, Smith noticed that a chain supporting part of the machinery was fractured. He climbed on to the machine to investigate but his left arm became entangled in the driving band, which was revolving about a hundred times a minute. Smith was dragged around the band, his neck scarf wound round the shaft and he was slammed against the roof of the room at every revolution. When Smith was extracted and taken to the General Hospital it was found that he was suffering from shock with several fractures of the arm, wrist and foot. The next day, Smith suffered convulsions, dying later that morning. The inquest found that Smith had no business trying to repair the chain and returned a verdict of accidental death.

15 FEBRUARY 1864 The Old Trees Inn, Hockley Hill, was in a terrible state of disrepair and the new owner decided to demolish the old building and erect a new one in its place. At about half past five this Monday afternoon, the workmen were engaged dismantling the gable-end when a wall suddenly and without warning collapsed into the garden of the premises of J. Price next door. Eleven-year-old Alfred Price, who was in the garden at the time, was buried under the bricks and rubble, and although workmen quickly rescued him, he was already dead. The inquest jury decided all care and attention was taken by the workmen and returned a verdict of accidental death.

16 FEBRUARY 1875 When the body of Harriet Latham, servant to Mrs Warner of The Avenue, Acock's Green, was found in the Warwick and Birmingham Canal near Yardley, police immediately suspected foul play. The nineteen year old, who three weeks earlier had disappeared while running an errand, was naked, had gashes across her body and her throat was cut. No reason could be given for Harriet to have wished to harm herself but the possibility could not be ruled out and the post-mortem revealed that the marks on the body were inflicted after death and Harriet had probably been embedded in the mud with the propellers of passing boats caused the terrible injuries. The inquest jury returned a verdict 'found drowned' but there was no evidence to show how Harriet came by her death.

17 FEBRUARY 1883 At about nine thirty this Saturday morning, Charles Ben Johnson from Ford Street, Hockley, was admitted to the General Hospital suffering from dreadful leg injuries. Johnson, a thirty-year-old shunter for the Great Western Railway Company, had been working at Snow Hill Station moving carriages when a passing train knocked him down under the moving wheels. His left leg was completely smashed from the middle of the thigh downwards, his right leg was crushed just above the ankle and he sustained a compound fracture of the right thigh. Despite prompt medical attention, Johnson died the same day from shock. The inquest returned a verdict of accidental death on the married father of one, just one of many deaths in similar accidents.

18 FEBRUARY 1833 This day saw the death of twenty-five-year-old mason William Badger, the second man to die following an accident at Birmingham Town Hall on 26 January 1833. Four workmen were engaged in erecting the roof of the Town Hall, hoisting part of it with a block-and-pulley system when the hook broke in two. The attached masonry fell to the ground from over 60ft, tearing the crane from the top of the opposite wall, which struck several of the men and precipitating four from their scaffolding. Two men escaped serious injury but thirty-eight-year-old father-of-two John Heap landed on his head, crushing his skull into his brain so that he died two hours later. Badger's ankle was badly fractured and, when he reached the hospital, part of the leg was amputated. He initially seemed to be making a good recovery but infection set in. The two men were buried together at St Phillip's churchyard where a monument was laid to remember their loss.

19 FEBRUARY 1835 On the evening of 16 February 1835, sixty-year-old William Painter was returning to his home in Ravenhurst Street, Bordesley, after spending the day in Birmingham. As he reached the parsonage ground in Smallbrook Street, four men suddenly attacked him and violently robbed him of his watch. Painter was able to stagger to the Rose and Crown public house and was conveyed home suffering from a broken jaw and a severely bruised neck. Over the next few days, Painter's throat and tongue became swollen and inflamed. The affliction progressed to his lungs and eventually killed him this Thursday evening. Two days later, twenty-year-old Benjamin Jones and twenty-three-year-old William Knowles were arrested when they tried to sell the watch at The Hole in the Wall public house, Camp Hill. Knowles, a known criminal, quickly realised that they would be charged with murder and told the police that he had been a bystander in the affair. Knowles named twenty-nine-year-old William Dolman, twenty-one-year-old Nathaniel Hedge and John Gough (who was just fifteen years old) as Painter's attackers; Jones had merely been with him to sell the watch. The men named by Knowles were quickly apprehended and sent to trial at Warwick Assizes in April 1835 for the wilful murder of William Painter. The damning evidence of Jones and Knowles meant that the three prisoners were found guilty and sentenced to death. Due to his tender years, Gough's sentenced was commuted to transportation for life but Dolman and Hedge were executed at Warwick Goal. Hedge died quickly but Dolman was seen to struggle for a while before death.

20 FEBRUARY 1877 A quantity of freshly brewed beer was 'working' in the cellar of the Cock and Pheasant, Nechells Park Road, Birmingham, and after the house closed, landlord William Butler and his thirty-four-year-old wife Elizabeth Hannah went down at different times to see how it was getting on. At about five o'clock on this Sunday morning, Mr Butler woke and realised his wife was not in bed. He went to the cellar where he was horrified to find Elizabeth lying senseless at the bottom of the steps. A doctor was called but the mother of four was dead, poisoned by the fumes from the beer.

21 FEBRUARY 1863 When thirty-six-year-old spoon polisher Frederick Newey returned to his home in Livery Street at about ten o'clock this Saturday night, he was intoxicated. He immediately began quarrelling with Mary Scott, the woman with whom he cohabited and the mother of his three-week-old daughter, Ann. Newey left but Mary, fearing his temper, decided to sleep in a different room when going to bed. He came back at about half past twelve and tried to drag Mary from the room by her hair. However, Mary resisted and Newey started to kick her. One of the kicks hit Mary on the arm where she was holding their baby daughter. Little Ann was caught on the head by the flying boot and knocked to the floor. The infant died within minutes and

Newey was arrested for her manslaughter. At Warwick Assizes, on 26 March, Newey denied harming Ann but the jury found him guilty and he was sentenced to twelve months' imprisonment with hard labour.

22 FEBRUARY 1873 This Saturday evening, after being discharged at the police court for the fifty-seventh time for drunken behaviour, thirty-four-year-old Ann Vale was crossing Great Lister Street when a cab horse knocked her down. Ann was taken to the General Hospital but, when it was found she was suffering only minor injuries, Police Constable Cottrell took her to the police cells at Moor Street Station, as Ann was totally inebriated. The next day Ann complained of chest pains and, despite medical assistance in her cell, she died on 26 February. At the inquest, Ann's husband said she had been a drunkard for fourteen years and would pawn everything in the house to get money for a dram. The post-mortem revealed a severe abrasion on her chest but death was attributed to congestion of the lungs brought on by excessive drinking and exposure to the cold. The jury returned a verdict in accordance with the medical evidence.

23 FEBRUARY 1872 A frightful and singular accident occurred this afternoon at the establishment of Messrs Morewood & Co., galvaniser in Wiggin Street. Eighteen-year-old George Bradley, eighteen-year-old Kain Marks and forty-four-year-old George Spelling were working near a large pot of molten metal when something fell from the roof into the pot, splashing the boiling metal over the three men. Spelling received only minor burns but Bradley and Marks were burnt to the bone on their arms, legs and uncovered chests. The three men were quickly removed to the Queen's Hospital where Spelling and Marks were admitted and remained for several weeks.

24 FEBRUARY 1891 On 4 February 1891, fifteen-year-old James Underwood and nine-year-old Robert Carswell, who were both inmates of the Gem Street Industrial School, were working together when Underwood decided Carswell wasn't working hard enough. Without warning, Underwood picked up a broomstick and hit the younger boy over the head. The blow fractured Carswell's skull and meant a two-week stay in the hospital and an operation. At Birmingham Police Court on this day, Underwood's mother blamed his attitude on a speech impediment that meant he was constantly teased but the stipendiary felt Underwood deserved fourteen days' imprisonment on top of the two weeks he had already served in custody. The master of the Industrial School told the court that Underwood would not be welcomed back.

25 **FEBRUARY 1884** William Jones and his wife Sarah of Camden Street were charged on this day at Birmingham Police Court with having wilfully neglected to provide clothing and food for their three children, to the endangerment of their lives. A relieving officer, who visited the home on 18 February, reported that their only furniture consisted of one chair, one table, a lamp and a few rugs. Both parents were drunk and eighteen-month-old Florence (who weighed less than 8lb) was lying asleep on a piece of coarse sacking that was saturated with water. All of the children were literally starving but William protested he could not help it and the children were 'as fat as pigs'. The magistrate said it was the most shocking case he had ever heard in court and sentenced William to three months' imprisonment. Sarah was discharged as the Bench believed she was acting under the influence of her husband.

26 **FEBRUARY 1887** This Saturday evening, Colonel George Newton Fendall left his barracks in Shrewsbury, telling his friends that he was going to the opera house in Birmingham. By twenty past ten, however, fifty-eight-year-old Fendall was at Redpath's liquor bar in Bull Street in the company of known prostitute, twenty-year-old Theresa Rooney. Shortly before eleven, the extremely drunk colonel was seen entering Theresa's house at No. 3 Court, No. 1 House, Bagot Street. At approximately half past eleven, a cab travelling down Lancaster Street was hailed by Theresa who asked the cab driver, William Vernon, to come to Bagot Street. Entering the house, Vernon found Fendall unconscious on a sofa, bleeding profusely from a head wound that Rooney said had occurred when the colonel fell in the street. Fendall was taken to Birmingham General Hospital but died early Sunday morning and Theresa was arrested on suspicion of murder as the wounds were not consistent with a fall; Fendall had more than thirty bruises and cuts on his body. Theresa's lover, twenty-four-year-old Joseph Lester, was soon also taken into custody; he had been spotted at Bagot Street at the time of the incident and had later taken Fendall's coat to his parents. The couple denied attacking Colonel Fendall or stealing from him. Nevertheless, their stories were inconsistent and it was felt that there was enough evidence to charge the pair with wilful murder. On 20 May they were tried at Warwick Assizes but the jury believed the death to have been accidental and found the couple guilty of manslaughter. The judge, after expressing dissatisfaction at the verdict, sentenced the pair to three months' imprisonment with hard labour. Soon after their release Theresa and Lester married at St Chad's Roman Catholic church but continued in various criminal activities for several years.

27 FEBRUARY 1874 James Aspinall, a licenced victualler in Pinfold Street, was used to removing customers if they crossed the line, so when twenty-three-year-old labourer Solomon Bayliss used bad language, Aspinall had no hesitation in throwing him out. A week later, on 27 February, Aspinall left his father's house in Freeman Street to find Bayliss standing outside holding a cup. Without a word, Bayliss threw the contents of the cup into Aspinall's face before running away. Almost immediately, Aspinall felt a burning sensation on his skin, eyes and mouth. Neighbours, seeing him in agony, rushed him to a nearby surgeon and it quickly became clear that nitric acid was the cause of Aspinall's torment. By then, however, much of the lining of his mouth was destroyed, his eyelids were badly damaged and his skin excoriated. Tried before Warwickshire's Lent assizes, Bayliss told the court that he had found the acid in a jar and had not thrown it at Aspinall until the victualler struck him, but the jury found him guilty of grievous bodily harm and Bayliss was sentenced to fifteen years' transportation.

28 FEBRUARY 1861 At about nine o'clock this Thursday evening, Mrs McCarty knocked on the door of her neighbour James Brown at his home in Henrietta Street with a stranger who was crying piteously. Mrs McCarty explained that she had found the young woman at Snow Hill Station and the poor girl needed their help. The stranger told them that she had been seduced by a young man who had since deserted her. She had found out that he was in Birmingham and had contacted him to say she had given birth to twins. The girl admitted that this last wasn't true and that she was trying to get money from him as she was now ruined. Unfortunately, a friend, who had agreed to loan her some babies, had let her down. James, taking pity on the girl, told her that she could use his four-week-old son as part of the deception and that his sister-in-law, Mrs Doon, had a boy who was six weeks old. The girl, with James and Mrs Doon in tow, took the babies to Noak's Refreshment Rooms in Union Passage where she told them that the young man was staying, and she went inside to speak to him. She came out a few minutes later to say that they were all to go to Snow Hill where the man would pay her £100. The group walked to Snow Hill Station where the woman suddenly vanished from the platform with the children. Distraught, James and Doon went to the police. Luckily a wet nurse in Harborne contacted the police two days later when she was asked to look after two baby boys and Eliza Davis was arrested when she returned to collect the children. At Birmingham Quarter Sessions, Eliza's defence explained that she was the wife of a medical man in Birmingham but suffered from mania and the child stealing was due to derangement; the jury, believing this, acquitted Eliza but she was detained to assess her long-term sanity.

29 FEBRUARY 1876 In order to facilitate the shipment of the patent manure manufactured near the Corporation Wharf in Shadwell Street, a building was being constructed near the canal basin. On this Tuesday afternoon, a number of workmen were standing on temporary scaffolding inside the building, affixing the iron roof, when without warning the roof collapsed. Five workmen managed to escape injury but three were not so lucky. Twenty-nine-year-old John Lloyd from Wolverhampton was crushed by the ironwork and died instantly from a compound fracture of the skull, while thirty-eight-year-old James McCale was so shockingly mutilated that he died immediately after reaching the General Hospital. A third man, John Watkins, was lucky to escape with a broken collarbone and was allowed home. At the inquest it was decided that one of the iron girders had broken so the weight of the roof was not supported; a verdict of accidental death was returned on the two men.

MARCH

1 MARCH 1891 Raymond Geary was only ten weeks old when he died on 13 March. The doctor, who attended the child just before his death at his home in Love Lane, found Raymond suffering from whooping cough, weighing less than 5lb and covered in sores. At the inquest, Raymond's mother, Ellen Geary, told the court that on the evening of 1 March, John McHugh, her partner and Raymond's father, had locked her and Raymond out of the house for several hours in the cold and this had caused the baby to develop a cough. McHugh said Geary left the house of her own accord and he went to bed not expecting her to come back later. Although the inquest jury returned a verdict of death from exhaustion, accelerated by whooping cough, the coroner expressed his opinion that the illegitimate child was allowed to starve to death by its brutal father, McHugh. McHugh was not legally Raymond's father and could not be called into account but the coroner censured Geary for her unfeeling behaviour.

2 MARCH 1869 At Birmingham Police Court on this day, thirty-two-year-old spring maker Thomas Crosby, nineteen-year-old Bridget Cummings, sixteen-year-old spoon polisher Mary Jane McManus and fifteen-year-old spoon polisher Mary Hope were charged with assaulting thirty-seven-year-old locket maker Elizabeth Coney and stealing a necklace and money from her. On the evening of 1 March, Coney was walking along John Street when she saw a large group of men and women standing together at the corner of London Prentice Street. When they saw Mrs Coney, the three accused women 'set upon' her, taking her purse and necklace before Crosby came up, knocked her down and savagely kicked her. At the trial it was revealed that Coney had given evidence against John Hope (nicknamed 'Bonner') at the last sessions and three of the accused were his friends or relatives. Several witnesses were called, an alibi was provided for McManus and she was discharged but the others were sentenced to two months' imprisonment each. On leaving the dock, Cummings threatened to 'silence' Coney. The stipendiary immediately placed Cummings in the dock again and ordered her to find two sureties of £5 each to keep the peace or be imprisoned for another three months. This had the effect of stopping Cummings' tongue but she left the dock with a significant nod directed at Elizabeth Coney.

3 MARCH 1883 The Birmingham Proof House in Banbury Street was established to provide a testing and certification service for firearms. On this Saturday morning, twenty-nine-year-old George Thornhill was working in the ramming room where he would ram the charges into the barrels before firing them off. It is believed that as he was ramming a breech-loading rifle the gun slipped and the firing pin struck the floor, causing the cartridge to explode. The charge caught the married father of three

square in the face, completely shattering his skull and blasting his brains across the room. Thornhill, of Great Russell Street, was described as a very steady workman at his inquest, where a verdict of accidental death was recorded.

4 MARCH 1876 Sixty-year-old button maker Isaac Elwell was well known around Pritchett Street for his drunken habits. Elwell, who had separated from his wife some time ago, was living with thirty-six-year-old Mary Boswell but they quarrelled on this Saturday night and Elwell turned her from the house. The next morning, Elwell was found dreadfully injured, the floor of the kitchen covered in blood and fragments of flesh, and his right arm so severely mutilated that the bone was clearly visible. Neighbours rushed him to hospital but he died within half an hour from blood loss. An old clasp knife was discovered under Elwell's body, which was clearly the murder weapon. Mary Boswell was arrested on suspicion of causing Elwell's death but she said he had been well when they parted. The inquest jury, finding no evidence to link Bowsell to the killing, returned a verdict of murder by some persons unknown. The murderer was never found.

5 MARCH 1883 At about ten o'clock this Monday evening, Thomas Astle from No. 4 House, No. 10 Court, Barn Street, was in Bradford Street when he saw a crowd of people gathering around Samuel Pipe and his common-law wife Ann, who were arguing with each other. When wood turner Samuel went to strike Ann, Astle intervened and received a violent blow from Pipe, who then ran away. Astle returned home but, realising he had been stabbed, went to the General Hospital, where he remained for three weeks. The surgeon found a deep puncture wound and, on 16 March, Pipe was arrested. He denied all knowledge of the attack but Astle identified him and Pipe was committed for trial at Warwick Assizes where he was found guilty of unlawful wounding and sentenced to five years' imprisonment.

6 MARCH 1864 Mrs Greenhill was cleaning the attic floor at her lodgings in Park Street on 15 February when she heard screaming from the bedroom below. Rushing down, Mrs Greenhill was horrified to find her two-year-old son, James Greenhill, white in the face with his lips scalded, a small bottle lying by his side. When she was told that the bottle contained poison used for electroplating she gave James mustard in water and took him to the Queen's Hospital where he initially made good progress. Sadly, James weakened and died this Sunday morning; the post-mortem revealed that he had ingested nitrate of mercury and the inquest jury therefore returned a verdict of accidental death.

7 MARCH 1891 Although twenty-six-year-old operative electrician Harry Spears was greatly liked by his neighbours, it was well known that he became violent and argumentative when drunk. Much of his anger was directed towards his twenty-year-old wife, Annie, and their Saturday night quarrels were a regular feature at their home in No. 9 Court, Rea Street. On this Saturday evening, the couple began arguing as usual but the row escalated to such an extent that Annie ran into the court screaming murder. Several neighbours came to her assistance, including fifty-eight-year-old Catherine Gallagher who went into the Spears' house to pacify him. This seemed to be working until Harry suddenly caught sight of his wife and tried to throw a chair. Another neighbour wrestled the chair from Harry, which enraged him so much that he picked up the paraffin lamp from the table and threw it against the wall. Tragically, the lighted fuel hit Catherine and her clothing burst into flame. She ran into the court where several people, including Harry Spears, tried to douse the blaze but Catherine was badly burnt. She was taken to the Queen's Hospital where she died nine hours later. Harry was tried and found guilty of manslaughter at Birmingham Assizes; the jury recommended mercy as Harry had attempted to put the fire out and the judge sentenced him to eighteen months' hard labour.

8 MARCH 1864 Thirty-nine-year-old engine fitter Joseph Silk of Shakspere's Place, Booth Street, Handsworth, was working on Monday morning of 29 February in the 'erecting shop' at the Soho Foundry. Silk was using a planing machine to chip a spring beam for an engine when he got too close and his trousers caught in the machinery as it slipped backwards and forward. His right leg was pulled in and crushed up to the thigh. Fellow workers rescued Silk and he was taken to the General Hospital where his leg was amputated below the knee. Despite prompt treatment, the married father of three died of his injuries on 6 March. The inquest held on this day returned a verdict of accidental death.

9 MARCH 1881 On this day a sanitary inspector visited the premises of William Henry Wills, potted meat and saveloy merchant. The inspector was horrified to discover half a ton of putrid mutton and horse flesh; the latter meat product included the carcass of a horse which died of glanders (a disease that could be passed to humans; the acute form of which results in septicaemia and death within days). The diseased meat was being used to make a variety of products and Wills was using red ochre to give the food an appearance of freshness. Brought before the Birmingham Police Court, the magistrates were told by medical officers that Wills had a large business so 'it is horrible to think of the amount of concentrated disease and putridity which he may have distributed before the nature of his diabolical practices was at length found out'. After expressing their regret that they could not inflict a severer sentence, the magistrates committed Wills to three months' imprisonment with hard labour.

10 MARCH 1872 On the evening of 16 February 1872, fifty-five-year-old plumber Frederick Farley entered the premises of Goods, Marr and Co., bankers of Upper Priory, Birmingham, requesting change for a sovereign. When Farley asked to remain there until a heavy shower of rain ceased, James Marr readily acceded the request as he was well known at the bank. Mr Marr turned to leave the counter and at that moment Farley produced a long-bladed knife and stabbed the banker in the back, under his right shoulder blade. Mr Marr turned to protect himself and Farley stabbed at his chest, luckily catching a button on Marr's coat and causing the blow to glance away. Alerted to the attack, William Gilliver and his son Alfred tackled the assailant who pulled out a hammer wrapped in brown paper and attempted to hit them over the head, giving each a glancing blow on the skull. It took several men to subdue Farley and take him to the police station where he would give no reason for his actions. Early the next morning, Farley attempted to kill himself by cutting his throat with a lancet that he had hidden in his mouth but he was restrained and removed to the General Hospital. On this day, he was finally brought before the Birmingham Public Office charged with wounding and doing grievous bodily harm to Marr, William and Alfred. Committed for trial at the Warwick Assizes in July, Frederick Farley was found guilty of attempted murder. The judge put forward the view that Farley's objective was to murder Marr and commit robbery, and passed a sentence of penal servitude for life.

11 MARCH 1908 In February 1908, an accident at the Hamstead Colliery prevented the mine from operating fully in the following weeks. However, on the morning of 4 March 1908, thirty-nine men were working underground when a fire broke out some 600yds below the surface; fourteen men managed to get to the surface before fire and falling debris trapped the rest. Local miners almost immediately attempted to get down the shafts to search for the missing men but they were driven back by thick smoke. Even rescue teams with breathing apparatus failed to reach the miners and one rescuer, named John Welsby, was overcome by the heat and failed to exit the mine. Today, when the fumes

Hamstead Colliery disaster. (Author's collection)

had finally cleared, fourteen bodies were recovered. The rest were unearthed over the coming days, including one group found next to a message board on which was written 'The Lord preserve us'. A memorial of a coal tub, bearing the names of the dead men, was unveiled in Hamstead in June 2008.

12 MARCH 1865 On the morning of 6 March, twenty-nine-year-old nail caster John Sharples was walking along Lawley Street with his brother William when he tripped over. John was holding a large carving knife in his left hand and, unfortunately, he fell sideways on to the sharp blade, which penetrated his chest and inflicted a severe puncture wound. His brother took him to the General Hospital but John's injury quickly became infected and the bachelor of No. 7 Court, No. 1 House, Oxford Street, died on the 12th. The inquest jury returned a verdict of accidental death.

13 MARCH 1894 At the Birmingham Police Court on this day, forty-one-year-old galvaniser James Noake of No. 6 College Street, Spring Hill, was summoned for ill-treating his four children in a manner likely to cause them unnecessary suffering. James' wife Jane was subject to similar abuse and had spent several weeks at the Women's Hospital on account of his treatment. While she was away, James spent much of his time drinking and, when he did return home, he would often attack the children. The eldest child, fourteen-year-old Florence, testified that James had hit all of them with a strap while they were naked; including one-year-old Arthur. On another occasion, James threw the grate front at Florence and beat the children with his belt buckle. Eleven-year-old Jem said that his father usually returned home blind drunk and they were beaten about three times a week. All the children were seen with bruising on their body and faces, while Jane Noake said James acted like a dog. James denied all charges but it emerged that he had been convicted of assaulting his wife and neglecting his family several times and the magistrate had no hesitation in sentencing him to three months' hard labour and fined him £25.

14 MARCH 1884 When tailor and hairdresser Henry Badder of No. 6 Rea Street heard that his employee and lodger Samuel Farmer was feeling unwell this Friday, he sent his wife to see what was wrong. When Mrs Badder entered the sixty-three-year-old's room, she found that Samuel had inflicted several cuts on his stomach. Samuel admitted to cutting himself with a razor: 'I may as well tell you the truth. I had a rupture at the navel, and it pained me very much and I nicked it.' A doctor was

called who removed Samuel to the parish infirmary but he died later that day. At the inquest the jury returned a verdict 'That the deceased died from syncope, accelerated by fright caused by his wounds.'

15 MARCH 1869 On his way to Wolverhampton this Monday morning, thirty-five-year-old groom John Smith (also known as 'Irish Jack') was standing at Handsworth Station. Needing to cross the tracks to catch the Wolverhampton train, Smith jumped off the platform and attempted to cross the line right in front of a goods train. The engine struck Smith on his side, slashing his ribs and head in a frightful manner before throwing his dead body on to the platform. At the inquest it was decided that Smith, who was rather short-sighted, had heard the warning whistle from the goods engine and, believing it to be his own train, had crossed without being aware of the danger. A verdict of accidental death was returned with a recommendation that a bridge should be erected over the line for the safety of passengers.

16 MARCH 1891 The hearing of the charge against thirty-three-year-old Louisa Stead of Clevedon Road, Balsall Heath, for cruelly ill-treating her twelve-year-old son Thomas continued on this day at Balsall Heath Police Court. In December 1890, a neighbour had seen Louisa strike Thomas twice with a poker and when he cried, hit him again with a cane saying that she would give him something to cry for. Over the next few months, Thomas was constantly covered in bruises around the face, head and back but his mother either attributed them to rough play or marks she had given due to Thomas' disobedience. The prosecution doctor said the injuries would have caused the boy unnecessary suffering; the Bench agreed and sent Mrs Stead to prison for one month, giving custody of the child to his father.

17 MARCH 1894 This day saw the trial of Frederick William Fenton for the wilful murder of Florence Nightingale Elborough. Fenton, a thirty-three-year-old metal spinner, had been courting twenty-four-year-old barmaid Elborough for several months. They had recently decided to marry and the couple were excitedly preparing for their life together. The nuptials were set for January 1894 and Fenton had already taken a house and was looking to buy furniture. However, all was not as it seemed, for Fenton was spending far more than he earned and was falling into greater and greater debt. On the evening of 12 December 1893, Fenton called for Elborough at The Plough and Harrow in Hampton Street, where she

lived and worked. She went into the kitchen, where Fenton pulled out a revolver and shot her several times before turning the gun on himself. The pair were rushed to the General Hospital where Fenton made a full recovery but Elborough succumbed to her injuries on Christmas Eve. At Birmingham Assizes, Fenton was tried and found guilty of the wilful murder of his fiancée. Throughout the trial he could give no reason for the killing and was executed on 4 April 1894 at Birmingham without making any further statement.

18 MARCH 1860 The beer was flowing in Cheapside on this Sunday night, so perhaps it was inevitable that a fight would break out sooner or later. A number of Irishmen, in a state of intoxication, began attacking each other but during the ruckus, labourers Patrick Morris and John Toy were seen to attack an 'old enemy' named Thomas Kennedy with a poker, hammer and belts. As the two men laid into Kennedy, he collapsed to the floor with serious head and chest injuries, but they continued to kick him until they were pulled away. Some of his friends conveyed Kennedy to the hospital where he died within hours without regaining consciousness. Morris and Toy were arrested and charged with manslaughter at Warwick Assizes where they were found guilty and sentenced to six months' imprisonment each. The two prisoners showed no emotion as they were taken away.

19 MARCH 1894 After suffering from heart and chest problems during the spring of 1893, thirty-three-year-old Alice Ada Clewer's health had slowly improved. Alice, who lived at No. 12 Court, No. 2 House, Clifton Road, Aston, was unable to look after herself and relied on husband Elijah to bring food during the day. However, Elijah took to spending much of his earnings on drink so Alice often went without food and the conditions in the house became squalid. Alice's sister came to live with the couple but seemed to find nothing amiss in the family's living conditions and refused to send for a doctor as her sister's health deteriorated. On 17 March 1894, Elijah was arrested for debt but it was already too late for Alice, who died early on 19 March from natural causes exacerbated by neglect and starvation. The doctor, who was called to view the body, was shocked to find it laid out on a table downstairs but the bed had been destroyed due to infestation. Alice's body was extremely emaciated and neglected. Her hair was matted and the eyelids were practically glued together with filth. She was wearing a few ragged articles of clothing and her bones could be clearly distinguished through her skin. At the inquest, the doctor said that in his thirty years' experience he had never seen a more deplorable case and the coroner was scathing to Elijah: 'You are standing

here a free man only because there is a technical difference between your case and manslaughter. I consider you are morally responsible ... and I hope you will be held up to the odium which you deserve.'

20   MARCH 1893   On 15 March, Thomas Hughes of Bon Marche, Steelhouse Lane, purchased a mare which he had been assured was quiet and broken to shafts. Happy with her behaviour throughout the following days, the mare was taken to Old Square this Monday, where she was attached to a float. However, just at the corner of Snow Hill and Steelhouse Lane, the horse suddenly bucked and the bridle broke. The two drivers, Henry Ankcorne and James Meades, tried desperately to control the horse but she broke free and galloped wildly down Slaney Street. At the bottom of the street, thirty-year-old Jane Twissell was pushing her nine-week-old daughter Amy in a perambulator across the road. Before she could get out of the way, the mare slammed into Jane, the shaft pinning her to the wall, then hit the perambulator which threw Amy to the floor. Jane suffered serious internal injuries and died within minutes while Amy died of a fractured skull shortly after admittance to the General Hospital. A verdict of accidental death was returned for Jane and Amy but it was felt that the harness had not been fit for purpose and on this evidence Jane's husband Henry Twissell, a fifty-nine-year-old brass caster, later sued Hughes for damages and was awarded £150. The horse, which broke its back smashing through a wall, was destroyed.

21 **MARCH 1871** When forty-year-old James Bland suffered one of his regular fits at the Borough Lunatic Asylum on 20 March, the night attendant put him back to bed in No. 5 ward. However, when the attendant returned to check on Bland at four o'clock this Tuesday morning, he found another patient – Charles Pearce – standing over Bland's bed with a cane chair raised above his head. When Pearce began ranting, 'They have murdered my wife, and I'll murder the lot.' the attendant wrested the chair away from him, but it was obvious that Bland had already been beaten around the head. A doctor was called and saw that James was more seriously injured than first believed, with bleeding from the left temple, cuts across his forehead and a piece of chair leg protruding from his skull. Brandy was administered but Bland lost consciousness and died a few hours later. The coroner's inquest heard that neither Bland nor Pearce (both residents at the asylum for several years) were known for violence and it was unlikely Pearce knew the consequences of his actions. Despite the evidence, Pearce was committed for trial at Warwick Assizes in July 1871, charged with wilful murder. At the hearing it emerged that Pearce was in Broadmoor Criminal Lunatic Asylum where he was judged to be insane, so the trial was deferred indefinitely.

22 **MARCH 1882** In December 1881, after years of heavy drinking, thirty-six-year-old watch-case polisher Henry Jeffries of Holloway Head took the pledge and had remained sober ever since. However, on 21 March, Henry came home drunk, having spent all of the available money the family had. Desperate for money, his wife Emma pawned Henry's coat to buy food on this day but he took eight pence of it and again went to the public house. When he returned drunk later this evening, he went alone into a room, picked up a bottle of cyanide of potassium that he used in his work, and drank it. Antidotes were given to Henry but without effect and he died in agony the next day. At the inquest a verdict of suicide whilst in an unsound state of mind was returned on the father of six, whose eldest child was ten years of age.

23 **MARCH 1850** Messrs Macarte and Bell's American Circus was passing through Dale End on its way to West Bromwich this Saturday morning and eighty-year-old James Kedger was watching the proceedings with interest. At about eleven o'clock, the front waggon stopped for the purpose of allowing the one behind to take the lead. The driver of the second waggon was endeavouring to turn the horses' head when the rein broke; the horses became unmanageable and drew the vehicle on to the footpath in Masshouse Lane, right where Kedger was standing. The waggon pole crushed Kedger against the wall of a pawnbroker's shop, causing severe internal injuries; Kedger was immediately conveyed to the General Hospital but he died on the way. The inquest returned a verdict of accidental death.

24 MARCH 1852 William Kirk Martin, also known as William Le Trot, earned his living as an equestrian and posture maker for the circus. In September 1851, twenty-six-year-old William persuaded a couple in Cheltenham to let him adopt two of their sons, seven-year-old Charles Day and three-year-old John so they could learn the art of gymnastics, and an indenture was drawn up. Promising that the two boys would be well looked after, William took the brothers away and, on 22 February 1852, they arrived in Birmingham. William, a woman calling herself Mrs Le Trot and the boys took lodgings in The Great Gun public house, Duddleston Row, where William's shocking behaviour to John became apparent. The little boy was made to stand in the corner of the bedroom for hours when he failed to perform his balances and was beaten around the head and body when he couldn't hold his handstand. On 1 March, William was throwing the boy into positions when there was a terrible scream and Mrs Le Trot rushed out for a surgeon who found John dead in William's arms. The Le Trots said that the child had landed on his head while turning a somersault. William was arrested when witnesses testified to seeing Le Trot frequently shaking the child and even hitting John's head against the floor. Tried before Warwickshire Assizes today, the defence argued that William had been perfectly within his rights to train the child and could not be held accountable for any accident. However, all the evidence pointed to William causing John's death and he was found guilty and sentenced to twelve months' hard labour.

25 MARCH 1885 Readers of the *Birmingham Daily Post* on this day would have been shocked to learn about an extraordinary case that took place at the Birmingham Police Court the previous day. It seemed that thirty-two-year-old landscape artist Herbert Alpha Newey of Bulcher Street had, in July 1883, engaged twelve-year-old Mary Elizabeth Wood as a nursemaid to mind his children. According to Mary, Newey began to behave improperly towards her and this continued for several months until it became clear she was pregnant. After the birth of the child, Newey told Mary and her mother that 'he supposed he should have to pay for it' and wrote letters to that effect. However, when Newey made no attempt to provide for the child, Mrs Wood contacted the police. The Bench, after hearing the case, said Newey was a most abandoned scoundrel and, after ordering a payment of 5s a week, he was also sentenced to two years' hard labour. The recorder wished that the punishment of flogging was available as a deterrent for such criminals.

26 MARCH 1888 On 24 March, a group of men, including twenty-four-year-old William Mander, were standing talking together in Curzon Street when they overheard a loud dispute going on at the corner of Viaduct Street. Mander and one of his friends went over and saw a man quarrelling with a woman. When the man went to kick

the woman, Mander stepped forward to pull him back. At that the stranger turned round and said, 'You take it instead', stabbing Mander in the chest with a knife. As Mander collapsed to the floor, bleeding heavily, the man, described as an 'ill looking, bow legged dwarf', escaped. Mander was taken to the General Hospital but the blade had severed an important artery and he died early this morning from blood loss. Mander's attacker, twenty-two-year-old Albert Cowper, was arrested for wilful murder and tried at Warwick Assizes where his defence successfully argued that, as the two men were strangers and Cowper had been drunk, he should be found guilty of manslaughter. The jury agreed and Cowper was sentenced to ten years' imprisonment.

27   MARCH 1898   When Augusta Villa Robson, a twenty-five-year-old domestic servant, took lodgings at her house in Camden Street, Mrs Lee had no concerns. However, on 27 March, Mrs Lee became suspicious when Robson didn't leave her room and strange noises were heard. A doctor was sent for, who realised that Miss Robson had recently given birth, though there was no provision for a baby in the room. When pressed, Robson admitted there was a child and it was wrapped in brown paper on the ledge of her washstand. The doctor undid the parcel and found the body of a fully formed baby boy with a piece of cloth tied tightly round its mouth and a leather garter round the neck. Robson was arrested when the post-mortem revealed that the child had been born alive but then suffocated. At her trial on 6 August, she was found guilty of the wilful murder of her child and was sentenced to death but this was later commuted to seven years' imprisonment. With good behaviour, Robson was released in 1902 and went on to marry and have a family.

28   MARCH 1862   It was common practice for the waste ground at Highgate Hill to be used by gun manufacturers to test rifles. At about six o'clock this Saturday evening, Thomas Kimberley, William Pinner and John Riley Jackson were trying out a double-barrelled breech-loading rifle when a group of men came rushing up to tell them that a bullet had hit someone in Bissell Street some 700yds away. Nurse-girl Mary Ann Barnacle was walking along Bissell Street holding Charles Breakwell, her ten-month-old charge, when the bullet entered her hand, passed through the baby's abdomen and then into Mary Ann's stomach. The children were taken to a nearby house, where Charles died within minutes, and Mary Ann was conveyed to the Queen's Hospital in a critical state. At the inquest, Kimberley, who was actually firing the gun, expressed shock that the bullet travelled so far but he was committed for trial at Warwick Assizes on a charge of manslaughter while Pinner and Jackson were charged with aiding and abetting. The judge, however, felt the three had no moral guilt and merely shown ignorance in bullet trajectory so they were acquitted.

29 MARCH 1859 On 15 March, four-year-old Mary Ann Robinson was playing in the road near her home in Darwin Street when she was approached by ten-year-old Edward Gibbons who was holding out a cup of liquid. Edward told Mary Ann it was wine and suggested that she should drink it, but, when she refused, he threw the contents of the cup into her face. Mary Ann immediately felt a burning sensation on her skin and ran screaming to her mother, who took her straight to the General Hospital. The doctor told Mrs Robinson that the liquid was vitriol acid and Mary Ann might lose her sight. Gibbons was brought up before Birmingham Police Court on this day charged with maliciously assaulting the young girl. It was proven that Edward knew the corrosive qualities of vitriol since he used it when working on tortoise shell, but the Bench were unwilling to send him to the assizes, thinking a week's confinement would do him good. When Mary Ann's eyesight was saved her mother decided on punitive damages and compensation was agreed.

30 MARCH 1892 This day saw the trial of Michael Ford for the manslaughter of Alfred Richard Beasley. Fifteen-year-old Amy Harrison was employed by the Beasley family of No. 20 Bartholomew Row to look after their children, including three-year-old Alfred. On 13 March, Amy took Alfred and another child for an airing in their perambulator. As they reached Allison Street, they came upon some youths who were throwing stones in the air to see how high they would go. Amy shouted to the boys to stop but three took no notice, including seventeen-year-old Michael Ford, his stone landing on Alfred's head, drawing blood and rendering the child unconscious. As the youths ran away, Amy went back to the Beasleys and a doctor was sent for. Alfred didn't regain his senses but became delirious, dying in great pain on 24 March from meningitis caused by his skull fracture. Witnesses came forward who recognised Michael and he was arrested for the manslaughter of the little boy. Tried at Birmingham Assizes, Michael was found guilty but discharged on his father's recognisances.

31 **MARCH** **1885** As Michael Ireland was walking along Sheepcote Street with two friends this evening, a gang of men appeared and, without provocation, rushed at Michael. Nineteen-year-old tube drawer Peter Conlon hit Michael over the head with a poker and, as he fell to the ground, several men began kicking him. While he was still on the floor, eighteen-year-old brass caster Edward Hurley stabbed him in the stomach with a knife before the gang ran away. Ireland was rushed to the General Hospital and, although suffering from severe blood loss, prompt treatment saved his life. Conlon and Hurley were arrested and charged with common assault at the Birmingham Quarter Sessions on 28 May 1885; their defence was that they had not been present and it was a case of mistaken identity. The jury, however, found the two men guilty and they were each sentenced to four months' imprisonment with hard labour.

APRIL

1 APRIL, 1890 At about midday on Tuesday, 1 April, sixty-year-old farmer Samuel Gunn of Lyndon End, Sheldon, was in the Bull Ring when a Pickford & Co. trolley, driven by James Wooley and Edward Draper, began to descend the hill. Just as the Pickford's trolley reached St Martin's church the horse's harness became unfastened, startling the horse and causing it to bolt. Wooley managed to steer it around several vehicles but the trolley eventually collided with a lamp post, causing the horse to smash into Gunn's trap, the shaft penetrating Gunn's horse's neck. Samuel was thrown from the vehicle and into the path of the trolley, which passed over his head. He was taken to the General Hospital with a skull fracture but died a few hours later from lacerations of the brain. The coroner's inquest of 3 April found no evidence of culpable negligence and returned a verdict of accidental death.

2 APRIL, 1890 Henry Schoenoick was working as a barman at the Canterbury Music Hall this Wednesday afternoon when he was approached by twenty-six-year-old hawker William 'Bowey' Beard who demanded a free pass into the concert hall. Beard was denied entry but pushed his way inside anyway and made for the liquor vaults. He was quickly confronted by Schoenoick and reacted violently, striking him in the face and the stomach. Arthur Hyde, the stage manager, was called and they attempted to throw Beard out of the Digbeth exit of the hall. However, at that moment nineteen-year-old Agnes Cullis and twenty-three-year-old Alfred Rutter appeared. Rutter struck Hyde in the face with his fist, knocking him to the floor before holding him against a wall and thumping and kicking him in the head. Cullis and Beard joined in the assault with Cullis screaming, 'Settle him! Kill him!' and hitting Hyde over the head with the end of a brick.

Eventually the three attackers ran from the scene as witnesses rushed forward to help Hyde. He was taken to Queen's Hospital but expressed a desire to go home. By eleven o'clock he lost consciousness after vomiting large quantities of blood and doctors performed a trepanning operation. After reviving for a short while, Hyde died on Friday morning from bleeding on the brain caused by a fractured skull. The three who attacked him were arrested and charged with manslaughter at Warwick Assizes in August 1890. All three were found guilty; Beard and Rutter receiving seven years' imprisonment and Cullis was sentenced to five years.

3 APRIL, 1891 When twenty-year-old brass cabinet maker John Patchett married twenty-two-year-old Harriet Gamble in 1880 the marriage seemed a happy one. Within two years, however, the couple were struggling with Harriet's excessive drinking as she 'sank into a dirty, drunken and degraded woman, who neglected her children and

pawned everything she could lay her hands upon'. John initially tried to help his wife but after a while began to drink heavily too and the pair often argued. In March 1891, after a particularly violent quarrel, the mother of six left the family home of No. 14, Cumberland Terrace, St Luke's Road, and lodged with her in-laws across the street. On 2 April, John, after drinking at the Baltic Inn, Sherlock Street, returned home followed shortly by Harriet and the couple retired together, seemingly reconciled. However, at about one o'clock this morning a fight started and John pulled out a pocketknife, slashing Harriet across the throat and severing her carotid artery. Within seconds Harriet fell dead to the floor, still holding their six-month-old son in her arms. John left the house covered in blood and gave himself up to a policeman. He was tried for wilful murder at the Birmingham Assizes on 1 August but the jury, deciding that there had been sufficient provocation, instead found him guilty of manslaughter and sentenced him to fifteen years' penal servitude.

4 APRIL, 1861 William Webb, Robert Wright and James Macnulty spent the evening of 3 April drinking together. By four o'clock this Thursday morning the three friends were rather drunk but in good spirits and, according to Macnulty, they walked along Great Queen Street 'chaffing and larking and tapping at one another'. Wright and Webb, both in their early twenties, started to wrestle but, when they both fell to the floor, Wright complained that he could not feel his legs or stand. A nearby policeman helped take him to the hospital but he was found to have broken his back and Webb was arrested for aggravated assault. On 14 April, Robert Wright died of congestion of the lungs caused by his spinal injuries and an inquest was convened. The verdict was accidental death but Webb did not attend. After hearing of his friend's death, Webb suffered an epileptic fit and died on 17 April from congestion of the lungs caused by epilepsy.

5 APRIL, 1833 At Warwick's Lent assizes on this day sixty-five-year-old brass founder Abraham Dodd was arraigned for the murder of his thirty-three-year-old daughter Mary Dodd. A few months previous, on 18 February, Abraham had called on surgeon Mr Bellamy to visit Mary as she seemed very ill. Arriving at the Dodd residence in Windmill Street, the surgeon found Mary in a wretched condition, suffering from severe vomiting and agonising stomach pains. She was immediately removed to the workhouse infirmary but died within the hour. A post-mortem was preformed which revealed that Mary was in an advanced stage of pregnancy and her stomach contents contained arsenic. Suspicion fell on Abraham and it became apparent that he had been carrying on an incestuous relationship with his daughter, who had learning difficulties. Finding her pregnant, he had given her arsenic to cause miscarriage.

The coroner's inquest returned a verdict of wilful murder against Mr Dodd and he was committed for trial. However, with insufficient evidence to warrant a true bill for murder, Abraham was found not guilty and acquitted.

6 APRIL, 1898 After his marriage broke down in 1897, forty-year-old jeweller William Greaves Edwards moved to London to start afresh. On this afternoon, however, he appeared at his nine-year-old daughter Alice's school and asked her to spend some time with him. The girl's mother agreed to this but asked a neighbour to follow the pair in case William attempted to abduct the child. William and Alice spent a few hours wandering around Birmingham before going to New Street Station at about ten o'clock. They were standing on the platform when, as a train pulled in, William picked up his daughter and threw her on to the tracks. Before Alice could escape, the engine passed over her, cutting off both her arms and a leg, but amazingly she was not killed. William was arrested and seemed disappointed she was still alive, asking, 'Can't you give her some poison?' At Birmingham Assizes on 3 August, William was charged with having attempted to murder his daughter, which he did not deny, adding that he did not want Alice to become a prostitute like her mother. The jury found him guilty but believed him insane and recommended mercy on the grounds of the provocation he had received. Edwards was sentenced to ten years' penal servitude and was sent to Winson Green Asylum.

7 APRIL, 1871 Twenty-eight-year-old coachman Henry Parkinson lodged with his sister-in-law Catherine Moore in No. 15 Rea Street but the relationship was not particularly cordial. On this Friday evening Henry came home rather the worse for drink and, when Catherine remonstrated, he became violent, throwing furniture and ornaments around the room and profaning. Catherine, concerned for her safety, ran to another room but Henry broke the door down and struck her across the forehead with a plate, inflicted a severe cut. Henry was brought before Birmingham Police Court the next day charged with violent assault. He was sentenced to six weeks' imprisonment with hard labour when the stipendiary was told that Henry had been reckless in his conduct for some time.

8 APRIL, 1841 This day saw the coroner's inquest into the death of Mary Ann Barrows of Wolverhampton. On 31 April 1841, Mary Ann was crossing the street in Snow Hill when butcher John Hunt and his brother came riding 'very fast' along the road. John's horse knocked her to the ground and trod on her chest and legs, throwing him off in the process. Though injured, John and his brother immediately

procured medical assistance for Mary Ann and she was conveyed to the dispensary. Unfortunately, she died of her injuries on 6 April and John Hunt was arrested. At the inquest, John expressed his regret and offered to pay the family compensation and funeral expenses. The jury returned a verdict of accidental death and a deodand of 5*s* was paid to Mary Ann's family.

9 APRIL, 1881 Although Kate Moran had been lodging with forty-five-year-old labourer John Richard Phipps at his house in Doe Street, it was her intention to leave this Saturday evening. However, when Kate returned to the house this afternoon, she found John throwing her belongings outside and exclaiming that he would chuck her out in the same way. She attempted to go inside but John blocked the door, striking her several times with his fist, before stabbing her through the hand with a penknife. Kate was found unconscious in the yard and conveyed to the General Hospital for treatment while John was arrested. At Birmingham Police Court he was found guilty and fined £5.

10 APRIL, 1860 When James Gates arrived in Birmingham from London late on this Tuesday evening, he called at Mr Cheshire's liquor vaults in Lower Temple Street looking for lodgings. James was approached by twenty-two-year-old engraver Reuben Lee and a twenty-year-old prostitute named Betsy Shelton who offered to show him a place to stay in Hill Street if he would 'stand [them] a glass of gin'. He gratefully accepted their offer but, as the group were walking along Pinfold Street, Lee and another man suddenly pounced on James and dragged him into an alley. As Lee held him by the throat, Betsy and the other man rifled through his pockets until James managed to break free and shout for help. Lee and Betsy were quickly apprehended and tried at Warwick's summer assizes for aggravated robbery; found guilty they were each sentenced to four years' penal servitude.

11 APRIL, 1891 On 13 December 1890, Abel Guest (aliases Edwin Guest and Abraham Guest) needed money and told his thirty-five-year-old wife Agnes to pawn a pair of trousers for him. She did as requested but, knowing the money would be spent on drink, she gave him somewhat less than the full amount she had obtained. Later, Abel returned to his home in Kent Street North worse for drink and a quarrel began about the money. In front of their thirteen-year-old daughter Georgina, Abel struck Agnes, who was holding their two-year-old son John Edwin in her arms. Agnes fell to the floor, whereupon Abel picked up a paraffin lamp, throwing it at his wife. The flames set Agnes' dress alight and she and the child were badly burnt. They were taken to Birmingham General Hospital where Agnes and John remained for some time. At Birmingham Quarter

Sessions on 11 April 1891, Abel was charged with inflicting grievous bodily harm upon Agnes and John but Agnes denied that her husband had pushed her or thrown the lamp, instead claiming that she had begun the quarrel and struck the first blow. When Georgina also retracted her statement the jury had no choice but to acquit Abel.

12 APRIL 1884 Fifty-nine-year-old bricklayer's labourer Joseph Oliver of No. 4 Barn Cottages, Harbourne, decided to stay up smoking after his children retired to bed on this Saturday evening. Just before midnight, Joseph picked up the paraffin lamp from the table and began to ascend the stairs. However, halfway up he dropped the lamp, covering himself with oil. His screams woke his son and daughter, who rushed to the stairs to find their father engulfed in flames; Arthur Oliver threw a cag over Joseph to extinguish the fire but he was already severely burned. Joseph was removed to the Queen's Hospital but he died of his injuries on 22 April. The coroner's inquest returned a verdict of accidental death.

13 APRIL 1876 On this day the coroner returned a verdict of accidental death on thirty-nine-year-old stonemason's labourer John Lowey of No. 9 Court, No. 1 House, Weaman Street. On the afternoon of 11 April, John had been at work, building the new wing at the Exchange, New Street. At about three o'clock he was standing on the scaffolding and drawing up some stone when fellow workers noticed him suddenly stagger and fall over 30ft to the ground. John landed on his head, resulting in immediate death from a crushed skull and severe lacerations at the base of his brain.

14 APRIL 1888 Courting couple twenty-nine-year-old George Nathaniel Daniels and twenty-one-year-old Emma Elizabeth Hastings spent this evening together in the Golden Elephant, Castle Street, Birmingham, where Hastings' father was landlord. At about eleven o'clock, Emma Hastings went into the kitchen followed by Daniels and a few minutes later screaming was heard and the sound of shots. Emma's mother ran into the kitchen to find her daughter bleeding from a gunshot wound to the temple with Daniels standing quietly by the fireplace holding a revolver. Daniels was arrested and taken to the police station where he confessed to the shooting, saying he was trying to break off the engagement due to money worries but he loved 'the ground Emma walked on' and if she survived he would marry her. Hastings was taken to the General Hospital where it was discovered that a bullet had penetrated her brain; sadly she succumbed to her injuries on 20 April. George Daniels was tried for wilful murder at Birmingham Assizes on 4 August where he said he did not remember shooting Hastings and claimed that she had visited him while he was in prison. The jury did

not believe his plea of insanity, found him guilty of murder and he was sentenced to death. Daniels was hanged at Winson Green Gaol on 28 August, dying without a struggle just after eight o'clock that morning.

15   APRIL, **1876** Just before eleven o'clock on the evening of 12 February 1876, twenty-one-year-old labourer John Ellis entered The Roebuck on Ludgate Hill with nineteen-year-old John MacDermott and nineteen-year-old Thomas Lavelle. They asked for beers at the bar but the landlord refused to serve them as it was near closing time. A friend of the landlord, William Parker, tried to move Ellis and his friends towards the door but Ellis took exception to this and struck him in the face before producing a knife and attempting to stab William in the head. Police Constable Edwin Stephens arrived on the scene and took Ellis into custody, but MacDermott shouted for help outside, crying, 'You shan't take him!' A gang then entered the pub, took off their belts and began to attack PC Stephens. Other policemen arrived and arrested Ellis, MacDermott and Lavelle for assault and riotously assembling to disturb the peace. Tried at Birmingham Quarter Sessions on 15 April, the three men were found guilty when witnesses came forward to testify they had seen Ellis, MacDermott and Lavelle using their belts and throwing stones at police. Ellis was sentenced to nine months' imprisonment, Lavelle to three months and MacDermott to four months; on leaving the dock MacDermott laughed, 'I can do that on my head'.

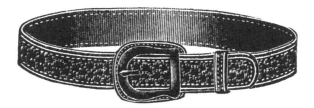

16   APRIL, **1850** This day saw the inquest on the death of twelve-year-old George Allen of Hampton Street. On 13 April, Allen was working at the gold chain manufactory of Messrs Goode & Boland, St Paul's Square, when he decided to sweep down his bench. Next to his workstation was a revolving shaft and, while he was clearing everything away, Allen's apron became caught and he was sent spinning around in the machinery; his head coming into contact with the floor several times. Allen's skull was fractured and one leg and both arms were badly mutilated; he was immediately taken to the General Hospital but died soon after. The coroner's jury returned a verdict of accidental death, with no blame attached to the employers since Allen had no business placing himself so close to the working machinery.

17 APRIL 1884 On 16 January 1884, Mary Ann Connor from Bartholomew Row was talking to her friend by The White Horse in Buck Street when the landlord called her in. Upon entering, Mary Ann was confronted by twenty-six-year-old Mary Ann Donoghue and her husband, who accused her of getting Mrs Donoghue drunk. When Connor replied that the landlord's wife had been drinking of her own free will,

Mrs Donoghue flew into a rage and picked up a kettle of boiling water. She threw it at Mrs Connor but missed and next grabbed a poker, smashing it over Connor's head. The police arrested Mrs Donoghue who said, 'Thank God, I have had the satisfaction on the black cow.' At the Birmingham Quarter Sessions on this day, Mrs Donoghue denied striking Mrs Connor and several witnesses testified that Mrs Connor had fallen over while drunk, but the surgeon at the General Hospital felt the wounds could not have been caused by a fall. The jury found Mary Ann Donoghue guilty of unlawful and malicious wounding and sentenced her to eight months' hard labour.

18 APRIL 1860 Sarah Pratt was considered a very pretty woman by those who knew her and this attracted a lot of attention, not always welcome. The twenty-four year old worked as a general servant for the Jackson's at The Swan with Two Necks Inn, Deritend, and it was there that she came to the attention of shoemaker Francis Price. From January 1860, Price paid his addresses to Pratt and, although it was clear that she was not interested, he continued to persevere. On this Wednesday morning, Price visited the house of an old washerwoman named Agnes Holmes who lived close to the inn and gave her 5s to lure Pratt to the house. Holmes went to the inn and told Pratt that her sister wanted her, and the unsuspecting Pratt set off to see what the problem was. As Holmes returned home some time later, Price rushed out covered in blood. Pratt was discovered lying on the floor, her head almost severed from her body, and Price was quickly apprehended, a bloodstained shoemaker's knife still in his pocket. He exhibited the greatest coolness and self-possession, merely saying that Pratt had positively refused his addresses. Tried at Warwickshire Assizes on 4 August, Price was found guilty of wilful murder and sentenced to death. He was hanged with some drama at Warwick Gaol on 20 August and the executioner, George Smith, had to pull Price's legs beneath the scaffold before he was launched into eternity.

19 APRIL, 1888 This Thursday evening saw the death of four-month-old Sarah Ann Maybury after she suffocated in blankets when put to bed at her aunt's house in Birmingham. This was the fourth death in four months for the unfortunate Maybury family. Sarah Ann's twin brother Arthur and her thirty-five-year-old mother, also called Sarah Ann, died in January 1888 during complications at the birth. Just weeks later the children's father, forty-two-year-old George Robert Maybury, was killed in a fall. The remaining six children of George and Sarah Ann were left orphans by this chain of tragic events.

20 APRIL, 1883 When two boys found a handcart left in Bordesley Street, Digbeth, this Friday morning, they decided to make a game of it. The boys invited some of the children from the street to sit on the cart so they could rock them violently back and forth. Four children, including twenty-month-old Leah Rees, climbed on to the cart to enjoy the ride. Tragically, the handle slipped from the boys' hands and the four youngsters were thrown to the road. The side of the handcart caught young Leah on the head, crushing her skull and causing a compression to the brain which resulted in death a few minutes later. The coroner at the inquest returned a verdict of accidental death after a scathing attack on any tradesperson who left such equipment on public streets without thought for the consequences.

21 APRIL, 1859 Twenty-one-year-old caster Edward Bridges of Slaney Street decided that twenty-three-year-old Amelia Davis was the girl for him. Although they were acquainted, Davis wanted nothing more than friendship from Bridges and so, when he asked her to live with him, she refused. Bridges took this rather badly and, on the evening of 16 April, he waylaid Davis in Slaney Street, dragged her into an entry and beat her so violently that her life was despaired of. Davis was removed to the workhouse and a deposition of the attack was taken in case her injuries proved fatal. Bridges was brought before Birmingham Police Court on this day, charged with violent assault, but Davis refused to give evidence and the case went no further.

22 APRIL, 1891 An accusation of neglect caused an officer of the Society for the Prevention of Cruelty to Children to visit Gem Street School on this day to examine eight-year-old Mary Ann Reeves and her six-year-old sister Emily. The girls, daughters of John and Emma Reeves of No. 3 Back of No. 124, New Summer Street, were in a shocking state. They were both emaciated, badly clothed and their heads were a mass of sores. What clothes they had were 'swarming with vermin' and the officer lost no time in charging their parents with serious neglect. On 30 April, father-of-seven

John Reeves appeared before the Birmingham Police Court and explained that the girls' condition was due to a hereditary disease. Mary Ann and Emily told the Bench that they did have plenty to eat so the magistrates decided to adjoin the case for a month to see how the girls were treated in the meantime.

23 APRIL, 1848 When thirty-two-year-old widowed father-of-three George Wheatcroft moved to New Canal Street, he was accompanied by thirty-six-year-old Ann Wheatcroft who claimed to be his new wife. The children, including eight-year-old German Wheatcroft, seemed fit and healthy but neighbours soon became concerned as they gradually lost weight and were seen covered in bruises. German and his younger sister Emily Sarah took to begging for food and, when neighbour Louisa Bland called at the Wheatcroft home, she found German tied to a box with a book in his hand. Ann told Louisa that the young boy had been learning his task for three days and 'he shan't have bit nor sup till he can say it'. Others witness recalled watching Ann stick a fork in Emily's head and taunt the children with lighted matches. When Ann corded German's hands and feet together, stripped him naked and beat him with a cane, the neighbours could take the cruelty no longer and they broke down the Wheatcroft's door, where they found the children 'like little skeletons'. German and Emily were removed from their parents care on 31 March but sadly German died this Sunday, his body unable to recover from its appalling treatment. George and Ann were arrested and tried for manslaughter at Warwick Assizes where George was found not guilty as no one came forward to testify seeing him treat his children unfairly. Ann, however, was sentenced to fifteen years' transportation to Van Diemen's Land; she died during the voyage and her body was buried at sea.

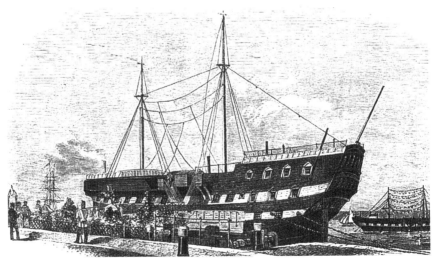

24 **APRIL, 1871** A quarrel, which took place in Clement Street, Ladywood, between neighbours Susan Wheeldon and Elizabeth Barnard, quickly escalated into a full-blown argument between the two families. This Monday evening, Elizabeth's twenty-two-year-old husband Charles Barnard went to the Wheeldon's house, kicking at the door and behaving in a violent manner. Twenty-four-year-old Charles Wheeldon rushed out of the house brandishing a knife, which he then proceeded to use against Mr Barnard. Charles Barnard fell to the floor with stab wounds to the chest, arm and face, and Mr Wheeldon was arrested and charged with malicious wounding. Tried at the Birmingham Quarter Sessions, Charles Wheeldon pleaded guilty and was fined 1s, ordered to enter into his own recognisances and to keep the peace for two years. Charles Barnard went on to make a full recovery.

25 **APRIL, 1895** Seventeen-year-old shoe finisher William Greasley of Bishop Street began arguing with a work colleague named John Marshall this morning and the quarrel turned violent. At one point, Greasley picked up a brick and threw it, intending to hit Marshall. Unfortunately, the missile hit a little girl who was standing nearby, causing serious head injuries. The child was taken to hospital and Greasley was remanded in Winson Green Prison. This evening Greasley was found in his cell in a deplorable condition, having hacked his throat with the edge of a tin can. The doctor stitched up his neck but Greasley said that he was subject to fits and did not know what he had done.

26 **APRIL, 1883** At Birmingham Police Court on this day, twenty-one-year-old press worker Emma Harris of Cecil Street was charged on remand with assaulting and stabbing Charles Chaplin of Ward Street. Chaplin had given evidence in the assault case between Crook and Donnolly, and had appeared for the prosecution while Harris appeared for the defence. Harris took against Chaplin for this reason and, on Monday, 23 April, when she came across him as he left a neighbour's house, Harris struck Chaplin with her fist, stabbing him in the head with a knife before saying, 'I will make you go and swear lies' and calmly walking away, throwing the knife as she did so. When arrested, Harris said, 'I will give him some more when I come out.' The magistrates committed her to the general quarter sessions in June 1883 where she denied using a knife, saying she had hit Chaplin over the head several times with a brick. Harris was found guilty of unlawful and malicious wounding and was sentenced to six months' hard labour.

27 **APRIL, 1861** On this Saturday morning, bricklayer James Morton left his wife Mary alone in their house in Devon Street, Aston. Fifty-year-old Mary was paralysed from the chest down and couldn't move without assistance so James made sure she was left comfortable in a chair by the fire. About an hour later Mr Morton returned to find

a scene of horror. Mary was slumped in the chair dead, her hands covering her face, her body completely charred and the greater portion of her clothing burnt to a cinder. It seems that Mary's dress had caught alight and she had been unable to save herself.

28 APRIL, 1891 Thirty-five-year-old labourer Henry Haines and his wife Sarah of Lime Grove, Walter Street, Nechells, were summoned to court on this day on behalf of the Society for the Prevention of Cruelty to Children for neglecting their unnamed son. The baby was born in February 1891, apparently in good health, but Sarah was a drunkard who the neighbours described as frequently in a 'muddled condition' and her house and the baby were allowed to get into an indescribably filthy state. Although the neighbours tried to help it was impossible to approach Mrs Haines due to her disgusting stench. When the child died on 24 March he weighed less than 3lbs, had been left unwashed for weeks and was consequently covered in sores. The stipendiary did not wish to send Henry to gaol as the home would then break up and the remaining children would be sent to the workhouse, so fined they Mr Haines £1 and sentenced Sarah to one month's imprisonment.

29 APRIL, 1914 Six-year-old Leslie Albert Stacey left his home in Wright Road, Saltley, to attend Highfield Road School this Wednesday morning as per usual. Although he was in good health when he left for school, that afternoon his mother received a message to say that Leslie was at the General Hospital seriously ill. When she arrived at the hospital, her son told her that he had been running down Highfield Road because a boy was after him. It later transpired that Leslie had in fact thrown a stone at another child as they left school, before rushing across the road into the path of a motor car. The driver had no chance to avoid the boy and the car drove over Leslie, crushing his ribs and causing fatal internal injuries.

30 APRIL, 1887 Residents at No. 6 Court, Ryland Road, were very suspicious of the friendship between fifty-nine-year-old wood turner Matthew Bannister and eleven-year-old Lucy Williams. On various dates in April, several neighbours saw Matthew and Lucy holding each other in an inappropriate manner and on this date some of the witnesses told Lucy's mother of their concerns. While Mrs Williams took her daughter to the Queen's Hospital, a group of female neighbours captured Bannister and drenched him under a tap before handing him over to the police. At Birmingham Quarter Sessions, where Bannister was tried for indecent assault, he told the jury that Lucy was at all times a consenting party; the assistant barrister said he had no doubt that was so but it was not a defence. The married father of two was found guilty and sentenced to nine months' imprisonment with hard labour.

MAY

1   MAY 1837 After many years of excessive drinking, fifty-three-year-old metal and rag dealer John Mathews suffered violent attacks of gout. For many months he had occasionally taken small quantities of the wine of colchicum seed to alleviate the pains. In April 1837, Mathews sent for three pennyworth of colchicum to Mr Southall's in Bull Street and received the medicine along with directions on the quantities that should be used in a day. However, on 29 April, Mathews had a bout of gout after becoming intoxicated and swallowed half an ounce of the medicine undiluted. He was soon seized with a dreadful sickness and violent pain, which lasted until he died this Monday morning at his home in Aston Street. The inquest held on 2 May found that John had no intention of taking his own life and returned a verdict of accidental death.

2   MAY 1850 On 14 December 1849, twenty-two-year-old Sophia Priest gave birth to an illegitimate child, whom she named Thomas, at her lodgings in Coach Yard, Bull Street. On 3 January 1850, Sophia told her landlady, Ann Jenkins, that she was taking Thomas to a nurse named Hannah, who she knew from a previous employer, and she was to pay 5s a week for the child to live there. On that same day, Thomas' father, Thomas Boot, saw her with the child near the house of her former employer, Mr Turley, in Grove Vale, Newton, Handsworth. Then, a few days later, Sophia returned to Turley's home and it was noticed that she visited the greenhouse in the garden. Sophia met with Thomas Boot in April and told him that, on her last visit to see baby Thomas, Hannah had informed her that the child had died of convulsions, to which Thomas Boot replied, 'Ah! It's better off then.' However, on 1 May, the decomposing body of a male infant was discovered in the stove flue in Mr Turley's greenhouse and, when it emerged that no child had been placed in Hannah's care, Sophia was arrested on this day. Sophia denied murdering her son, telling the police that she gave a stranger half a crown to dispose of Thomas. At Staffordshire Assizes in August 1850, Sophia's defence argued that it could not be proved that the body was that of Thomas Priest or indeed if Thomas was dead, and since the body was so decomposed, the cause of death could not be ascertained. The jury decided there was insufficient evidence to convict Sophia and she was acquitted of murder. It should perhaps be noted that Thomas was Sophia's third illegitimate child to have 'disappeared'.

3   MAY 1893 Although they had only married in October 1892, Walter Nutt Wormington and his twenty-three-year-old wife Ada were already extremely unhappy. Within six weeks of marriage, thirty-two-year-old Walter began striking Ada and this continued throughout the following months. On 3 May 1893, Walter arrived at their

home in Grove Lane and went to bed but when Ada followed the door was locked. When he eventually opened the door Walter began kicking his wife before dragging her around the room. Brought before Handsworth Police Court on 19 May for beating Ada, Walter said he had been greatly provoked, accusing Ada of spending time with another man. This was strenuously denied by Ada and the Bench fined Walter 40*s* with costs but refused to grant a separation order. Ada Wormington gained a divorce in 1894, citing adultery and cruelty on the part of her husband.

4 MAY 1841 As George Eccleshall left his house in Reservoir Lodge to walk along the dam to the engine house this morning, he noticed a hat floating in the water. After fishing it out he continued to work, but at about ten o'clock he saw a large object floating in the Edgbaston Reservoir near the wall. When he realised it was a body, George summoned assistance from the Sand Pits station house and between them they pulled out the body of a middle-aged man, money still on his person but with stones in his jacket pockets and a large head wound on the left side. It was clear the body had been in the water for some time. The inquest drew several witnesses who remembered seeing a man matching the deceased's description about three weeks before, who was being dragged along by three other men. A Mrs Herbert reported her young son seeing this and saying 'Mamma, I think they are trying to kill him, for they put a towel into his mouth, and he cried out "murder!"' None of the witnesses had felt any need to help or report this to the police. A surgeon, who examined the body, found a large quantity of coagulated blood on the surface of the brain and felt that the head injury had caused the death of the unknown man. The jury returned a verdict of murder by some person or persons unknown. The body of the man was never formally identified.

5 MAY 1882 Goldbeater John Woolley and servant Ellen Jennings had been keeping company for the last four years but – fed up with his drunken habits – Jennings finished the relationship in April 1882. On this Friday evening, Jennings was working at the Waterloo Tavern, Lower Priory, when a boy came in and told her that Woolley wished to speak to her outside. As soon as she went out, Woolley began to accuse her of seeing another man and, when she turned to leave, he pulled out a carving knife and struck her in the left breast with such force that the blade broke. Jennings fell to the floor, but luckily she was quickly conveyed to the General Hospital where she recovered from her injury. Tried for felonious wounding at Warwick Assizes, Woolley explained that he had been so drunk he could remember nothing of the incident. When he was found guilty, Jennings pleaded for leniency but the judge declared that Woolley could easily have killed her and so sentenced him to five years' penal servitude.

6 MAY 1840 Seventeen-year-old Josiah Lilly was apprenticed to a tradesman in Birmingham but, after falling in with the wrong crowd, absented himself from work and was sent to a house of correction. While he was incarcerated, the father of his sweetheart, nineteen-year-old Harriet Wright, forced her to break with Josiah. When he realised, Josiah took a bonnet and shawl of Harriet's to try and force her to see him. However, Harriet's father reported the 'theft' and Josiah was again arrested. Informed that Harriet would testify against him, Josiah expressed great bitterness towards her but she refused to appear against him and the charges were dropped. On this Wednesday evening, Josiah persuaded Harriet to meet him and the pair were seen arguing together at Walmer Lane Bridge which crosses Fazeley Canal. Early next morning the body of Harriet was found floating in the canal and Josiah was arrested for her murder. At Warwick Assizes in August 1840, Josiah denied killing Harriet, saying she had threatened to kill herself because of their relationship. The jury decided that Harriet had committed suicide and Josiah was acquitted.

7 MAY 1862 As Ellen Lowe of No. 21 Court, High Street, Bordesley, was in the yard pumping water this Wednesday afternoon, her six-year-old son Harry came running over, closely followed by publican Richard Taylor. When Taylor caught up with Harry he struck him on the back of the neck, telling Ellen, 'Missus, the children are always in mischief' before walking back to his home at the Rising Sun. Harry cried for a while but Ellen had little sympathy as he had been told by Taylor not to play in the bowling alley at the public house. The boy seemed unhurt by the blow but two days later began complaining of aching joints, becoming weaker and delirious before dying on 12 May. Witnesses at the inquest recalled seeing Taylor hit Harry with a clenched fist but a post-mortem revealed congestion of the brain, which the doctor did not feel could be caused by such a blow, so the jury returned a verdict of death by a visitation of God.

8 MAY 1860 Just before Christmas 1859, William White seduced twenty-two-year-old Mary Turner while promising to marry her. However, by April 1860, White accused Turner of seeing other men and having a venereal disease which she heatedly denied. Shortly afterwards, White told Turner that he would not marry her and was seeing another woman who he was going to make his wife. The estranged couple remained at the same lodgings in Barn Street but did not speak to each other except to argue. On this Tuesday evening, White returned home from work and was washing in the brew house when Turner suddenly appeared with a pistol in her hand and shot him in the hip. Arrested and tried at Warwick Assizes for grievous bodily harm, Turner admitted the charge but explained she had been driven to violence by White's cruel treatment. Character witnesses bore testament to Mary Turner's excellent character up until her unhappy connection with White and she was sentenced to eighteen months' imprisonment.

9   MAY   1864   A horse and cart were standing in Rea Street this Monday afternoon when the horse suddenly took fright and ran off down the road. Forty-seven-year-old James Ward of Lee Bank Road, who was in charge, ran after the mare and attempted to jump on the shafts to take control. However, as he did so, Ward slipped and fell to the ground. The wheels of the van ran over Ward's left leg, shattering the bones in several places. He was taken to the General Hospital but gradually declined, dying of his injuries on 21 June. An inquest jury returned a verdict of accidental death.

10   MAY   1880   Early on the morning of 1 April, eighty-three-year-old John Millard, an inmate of Birmingham Workhouse, woke and began moving around one of the men's dormitory. The noise of his walking sticks woke sixty-seven-year-old Bartholomew Flateley and he asked Millard to be quiet. Millard took offence and the two men exchanged 'words' before Flateley attempted to grab Millard and they both fell to the floor with Flateley on top. As they scuffled Flateley knelt on Millard's stomach and put his hands round his throat until he collapsed. Taken to the workhouse infirmary, Millard became increasingly ill. On 10 May, he died of peritonitis, which the doctors believed could have been caused by his violent altercation with Flateley. Tried for manslaughter at Warwick Assizes on 31 July, the jury decided that Flateley was not responsible for Millard's death and he was acquitted. Flateley remained in the workhouse until his death in 1897.

11   MAY   1891   At Birmingham Police Court on this day, Arthur Thompson of Bordesley Street was summoned for indecent assault on a minor. On the Sunday afternoon of 10 May, fourteen-year-old Emily Smith was walking through Union Passage when she was approached by Thompson and, before she could react, was pushed to the floor where he attempted to undress her. Luckily, Thomas Edkins was passing by and, hearing Smith's screams, went to her assistance. Thompson ran from the scene but Smith and Edkins recognised him and he was quickly arrested. The court sentenced Thompson to six weeks' hard labour and thanked Edkins for his behaviour, awarding him 5s.

12 MAY 1917 This Saturday afternoon, fifty-two-year-old carter William Massey, who lived at No. 2, back of No. 9 Sheepcote Lane, went to the army ordnance depot at Aston Goods Station with a load of bedsteads. Massey drew his lorry under a hoist and was in the process of unloading when it was decided that a bale of compressed straw needed to be lowered for the second floor. The word was given to stand clear and the bale was

being lowered when the binding wire, to which the hook of the lowering chain was fixed, broke. The bale, which weighed over 80lbs, fell, struck the lorry and bounced on to Massey. The carter was knocked down, breaking his breastbone and several ribs and injuring his spine. Despite prompt treatment at the General Hospital he died within hours and a later inquest returning a verdict of accidental death.

Looking back along the tracks towards Aston Station. (Author's collection)

13 MAY 1872 When thirty-year-old Humphrey Sullivan's wife moved out in April 1872, he was left to take care of his five-year-old son, Thomas, in the garret of a house in Bishop Street. Humphrey worked as a warehouseman and would often leave the boy alone all day when he went to work. Fellow lodgers revealed that they frequently heard Thomas crying throughout the day but at his father's return he would scream in fear. On the evening of 12 May, Humphrey returned home the worse for drink and attacked Thomas, beating his little body with his fists and giving him a black eye. This morning, lodger Selina Parker found the boy huddled and filthy in the corner of the garret and contacted the police. Humphrey was taken into custody and charged with violent assault at Birmingham Police Court where he admitted to the Bench that, in the heat of passion, he had knocked Thomas into the grate. In his defence, Humphrey claimed that his wife had stolen the child's clothing and he must work so had no choice but to leave the boy. However, when the court heard that Humphrey had refused the aid of a lodger who had offered to help care for Thomas, they sentenced him to two months' hard labour.

14 MAY 1884 At Warwick Assizes on this day, thirty-three-year-old railway clerk William Thomas was indicted for the wilful murder of twenty-nine-year-old Emma Jane Hollis. William lodged at Emma's coffee house in No. 182 Spring Hill and, while her

husband, Henry Herbert Hollis, was serving in St Helena with the Northamptonshire Regiment, he formed an improper relationship with her. However, on 19 March the couple quarrelled and Emma taunted William, saying that another man had replaced him in her affections. William, who was described as besides himself with rage, followed Emma into the kitchen, picked up a clasp knife and stabbed her repeatedly in the face and neck. Emma staggered into the street and, in front of horrified onlookers, died in the gutter. William was found in the kitchen, a self-inflicted neck wound clearly visible; he was rushed to the Queen's Hospital, where he made a full recovery. At his trial, William's defence argued that he had been severely provoked and was therefore guilty of the lesser charge of manslaughter. The jury agreed and he was sentenced to penal servitude for life.

15 MAY 1878 Living together at Great Russell Street, Newtown, fifty-four-year-old Sarah Coleman and fifty-year-old Joseph Taylor were often the worse for drink so, on the evening of 14 May, when Joseph's son John returned from work to find the couple intoxicated, he was not surprised. He left the pair and went to bed but, at about midnight, John heard a noise followed by shouts for help from Joseph because Sarah had fallen down the stairs. John found Sarah lying on the floor, bleeding and insensible, so he helped his father to carry her to the sofa before again retiring to bed. According to Joseph, he stayed with Sarah for a couple of hours before he went to bed but when he checked her at five o'clock on this Wednesday morning, Sarah was dead. The post-mortem showed damage to the front and back of the head, with a broken nose and arm; Sarah had died from a skull fracture. In the doctor's opinion the injuries were excessive for a fall down stairs and Joseph was arrested. Tried at Warwick Assizes for manslaughter on 7 August the jury felt there was not enough evidence and he was acquitted.

16 MAY 1890 Gunsmith Frederick Davis had been a loving husband and father to his five children until he began drinking heavily some eighteen months previous to this date. His wife Sarah Ann begged him to give it up and recently it seemed Frederick was attempting to do so and began working again. However, when neighbours witnessed the couple returning to their home in St Stephen's Terrace, Newtown Row, this Friday afternoon, it seemed that a drunken Frederick was carrying a shotgun. About twenty minutes later a shot was heard and Sarah Ann, blood streaming from her mouth, came running into the yard where she fell and died within minutes. Frederick made no attempt to escape and was arrested at the scene, crying that it was the drink and 'the woman aggravates you so'. The post-mortem showed that Sarah Ann was shot in

the back and the bullet had travelled through her ribs, gullet and windpipe before exiting the breast. Tried at Birmingham Assizes for wilful murder, Frederick told the court that he had shot his wife in the kitchen when she began reproaching him for his intemperate habits. Sentenced to death, Frederick was hanged at Winson Green Gaol on 26 August 1890; his death was instantaneous, although his neck was severely torn by the drop, with both the windpipe and carotid artery being severed.

17   MAY   1891   After the death of her child in 1883, forty-year-old Mary Ann Horsfall of No. 5 Court, No. 4 House, Bartholomew Row, was distraught. According to her husband, Joseph, she was never again 'the same in her mind' and had attempted to take her own life three times. Tragically, another of their children drowned in November 1890. On 17 April 1891, Mary Ann gave birth to her ninth child, a boy, but she was very ill after her confinement and was given to restlessness and complaining about the children. On this Sunday, Mary Ann got up and spent most of the morning walking up and down the stairs aimlessly. Then, at about quarter to twelve, she went into the room where the baby slept. Suddenly she shouted to her husband that she had killed the child and, when Joseph and their eldest son hurried in, they found her about to smash the baby against the bedpost. The two men grabbed the infant but it was already too late, the baby boy's skull was crushed from a massive blow, presumably caused by the bedpost. Mary Ann sat in the bedroom as a doctor was called, her manner wild and speech incoherent. She was arrested and charged with the wilful murder of her unnamed infant son but she was declared insane and removed to Broadmoor Lunatic Asylum in June 1891.

Broadmoor Lunatic Asylum. (THP)

18 MAY **1893** Twenty-nine-year-old labourer Charles Print arrived at his home in Lyndon Road, Sutton Coldfield, extremely drunk this Thursday evening and began arguing with his mother, Hannah Hickinbottom. The quarrel became violent when Print picked up a basin and struck Hickinbottom a violent blow across the head, causing several wounds that necessitated medical attention. Brought before Aston Police Court, Print was ordered to pay a fine of 10s and the doctor's fee or fourteen days' imprisonment; the court remarking at his cowardly behaviour in attacking a defenceless old woman.

19 MAY **1865** Early on this Friday morning, night soil man John Mills was engaged at his work in No. 8 Court, Bath Street, when he discovered a bundle completely buried in the human waste. He opened the parcel and was horrified to discover that it contained the dead body of a newly born boy. The police were informed and an inquest was held the next day. The surgeon, Mr Solomon, stated that his post-mortem revealed the body exhibited no marks of violence; the baby had breathed but whether before or after birth he could not say. The jury returned a verdict of 'found dead' and the unknown child was buried in a mass grave, his parentage never discovered.

20 MAY **1892** As the cable car reached Colmore Row, forty-nine-year-old painter William Roe, of Bridge Street West, made to alight. The guard asked if Roe wanted the tram to halt but William said he was fine and 'dropped off' the car. Just as he was crossing the line, however, another tram hit William and dragged him beneath the wheels. The tram was immediately stopped but it took three-quarters of an hour to fetch iron levers to raise the car and extricate William's body. His head had been crushed and his body was terribly mangled. The inquest returned a verdict of accidental death on the father of Lilian Roe, whose school helped raise money to ensure a decent burial on the unfortunate man.

21 MAY **1843** Market gardener James Williams was so devastated to find himself in pecuniary difficulties that in April 1843, and in a state of distraction, he stabbed himself in the stomach with a clasp knife. The wound did not cause severe injury so, only days later, the fifty-year-old threw himself into Hamstead Mill Brook but was seen struggling in the water and pulled out. Williams seemed to return to his normal self, but the stomach wound festered and, despite attention from a surgeon in Great Hampton Street, he died this afternoon at his home in Hockley Hill. The inquest returned a verdict of death from a wound inflicted while in a state of temporary insanity.

22 MAY 1850 When Ann Seaborn, a mother of three, found out that her twenty-four-year-old husband John was 'paying undue and improper attention' to another woman, she was devastated. On the afternoon of 20 May, John left their home at Primrose Hill, Great Lister Street, and Ann, sure he was visiting his mistress, was stung with jealousy. Picking up their youngest child, Mary Ann, Ann went into the garden where she flung herself and the baby into the well. The two other children were left alone until one of them finally went in search of her father and was able to tell him what had occurred. John and some companions rushed to the house where they extricated the dead bodies of Mary Ann and Ann from the well. The inquest on this day returned a verdict to the effect that Ann terminated her own and Mary Ann's existence while in a state of insanity; John was obliged to be protected by the police on his way home from the inquest.

23 MAY 1918 This Thursday afternoon, thirty-five-year-old labourer David Smith from No. 29 Twyning Road, Stirchley, was working at Kings Norton Metal Works, lifting one of the heavy metal doors off its hinges. The workman attached hooks to the door to lift it but, as it began to move, one of the hooks broke, sending the door back to its proper position. As it did so an iron lever struck Smith's legs, injuring one of his thighs so badly that it was found necessary to amputate his leg. Unfortunately, blood poisoning set in and Smith succumbed to his wounds. A coroner's jury returned a verdict of accidental death although several witnesses expressed their opinion that the hooks had not been strong enough.

24 MAY 1884 The mother of one-year-old Jane Barton decide to leave the baby with her three-year-old sister at their home at the back of No. 115, Adam Street, while she ran some errands. No one knows quite how but while their mother was out, little Jane fell head first into a pail in the kitchen, which contained about 2in of water, and before she could be pulled out, she drowned. A young woman who lodged in the house heard the older girl's cries and ran down only to find the baby lying by the side of the pail, dead. The coroner's court returned a verdict of accidental death.

25 MAY 1895 Albert James Grimshaw was at a public house in Aston this Saturday evening where John Sanders alias 'Mad Jack' was also drinking. Grimshaw, who came from Nechells, decided to leave but accidentally trod on Sanders' toes as he did so. Sanders took immediate exception to this and the two men began to argue before Sanders took out a large clasp knife from his pocket and drove it into Grimshaw's forehead. The blade broke through the skull and punctured 1in into Grimshaw's brain.

He was taken to the General Hospital but died three days later. Sanders was taken into custody and charged with wilful murder but when the case was taken before the Warwickshire Assizes on 24 July 1895, he was declared insane and ordered to be detained at Her Majesty's pleasure.

26 MAY 1896 In October 1894, George and Catherine Crowe of Cromwell Street were devastated by the loss of their twelve-year-old son John when, while trespassing on a railway line, he was knocked down by a train and cut to pieces. However, further sadness was to follow. On 23 May 1896 another son, twelve-year-old George Crowe, went to stay with his grandmother in Duke Street. This Tuesday afternoon, George was running down the entry when he suddenly slipped and fell, hitting his head on the ground. Bleeding heavily from the skull, George's injuries gave enough concern that he was taken to the General Hospital. Two hours later he died from a fractured skull and laceration of the brain. After expressing sympathy to the unfortunate parents, the inquest jury returned a verdict of accidental death.

27 MAY 1885 Twenty-two-year-old filer Thomas Lynocks of Green's lodging house, Park Street, and Ann Inslow were drinking heavily this Wednesday night when they began rowing as they walked along the street. The argument escalated and Lynocks picked up a brick, striking Inslow across the head and knocking her unconscious. Lynocks left Inslow insensible on the ground but witnesses took her to the General Hospital. At Birmingham Police Court, Lynocks was found guilty of violent assault and sentenced to four months' imprisonment with hard labour.

28 MAY 1883 A new theatre was being erected in Corporation Street and on this Monday morning thirty-two-year-old John Tapper of Osler Street was on the scaffolding, fitting some timber to the wall, when a brick was dislodged by another labourer higher up. A warning was shouted but Tapper was hit on the head by the falling brick, causing him to fall 20ft to the floor. Tapper was picked up unconscious and bleeding from a head wound, and taken to the General Hospital. The doctors diagnosed a skull fracture extending across from top to base and, when Tapper remained insensible, trephined his head but he died on Wednesday evening. A verdict of accidental death was recorded on the married father of one.

29 MAY 1868 When Mr Lilly set up a fog-signalling factory on land which stood a couple of hundred yards away from Saltley Training College, Cherry Lane, he made sure it was fully conversant with safety regulations. He could not have predicted, however,

that a lightning storm would hit with such devastating force this Friday morning, hitting the finishing shed and setting the roof alight. Some 300 gross of fog signals were in the building, representing over 43,000 single explosions. Before too long the roof fire began a train of explosions, which lasted almost two hours. Tragically, six girls were working in the shed; four ran out with clothing and bodies burning, one girl tearing off the flesh on her wrist in an attempt to stop the flames. The four girls (fourteen-year-old Emily Colden, twelve-year-old Emma Tandy, thirteen-year-old Eliza Lovell and eleven-year-old Mary Ann Essex) were conveyed to the General Hospital but nothing could be done for eleven-year-old Fanny Riddle and twenty-three-year-old Lizzie Reynolds. Their bodies were later discovered in a 'sickening state'. According to witnesses they looked like pieces of charred wood, with their arms and legs severed and in fragments. Sadly, Mary Ann Essex and Eliza Lovell also died of their injuries within twenty-four hours of the fire. The inquest, which was finally held in October so that the remaining girls could be questioned, returned a verdict of accidental death but suggested smaller quantities of gunpowder should be stored and a lightning rod fitted.

30 MAY 1882 On this Tuesday afternoon, thirty-year-old painter George Smith was 'having words' with his sister Harriet, who lived with him in Bishop Street South, when neighbour Sarah Tullett came over to remonstrate. George instructed Sarah to stop interfering but she refused to leave and George knocked her to the floor. She left the house but returned within a few minutes along with fellow neighbour Ellen Ingram who also began to scold George. This only enraged him further and George hit Ellen around the face, blacking her eye. Charged with assault at Birmingham Police Court, George argued that the two women had no right to get involved but the Bench ignored him and decreed a fine of £5 40s with costs.

31 MAY 1878 Twelve-year-old James Edward Strong and his brothers, nine-year-old Benjamin and four-year-old Charles, left their home on the afternoon of 30 May 1878 and went to the bank of the River Rea near Balsall Heath Road. The three boys brought a pram with them, which Benjamin and Charles were playing in when it suddenly rolled down the bank and pitched the boys into the water. James rushed to help his brothers but was dragged in by the weight of the pram; the boys' cries alerted a woman who was able to grab James but the other two boys were carried away and drowned. The inquest on this day returned a verdict of accidental death on the two young brothers.

JUNE

1 JUNE 1894 After living together at No. 7, back of No. 83, Great Francis Street, for three months, twenty-one-year-old Mary Withey left William Henry Harvey (alias Joseph Harvey) in May, unhappy with the frequent quarrels and Harvey's brutal behaviour. Harvey, a twenty-five-year-old painter, took the separation badly, threatening to shoot Withey with a gun. Terrified for her life, Withey sought police protection but the threat seemed an empty one as Harvey made no further attempts to intimidate her. On this Friday, Withey was at work at Messrs Benson's brass founders when William appeared and begged her to walk with him, expressing sorrow for his earlier behaviour. The couple were walking in a field near the Birmingham Corporation sewage farm at Saltley when Harvey suddenly pulled out a clasp knife and repeatedly stabbed Withey in the breast and head before throwing her to the ground where he proceeded to kick her until she was dead. Harvey then calmly walked up to some men and told them what he had done: 'I intended to kill my missus and now I'm satisfied ... that was how I wanted to see her die.' Harvey was arrested and accused of wilful murder but on 6 June he became ill after taking poison and died in great agony the next day in Birmingham City Gaol.

2 JUNE 1879 Twenty-nine-year-old Sarah Turner was employed as a cook for Lieutenant Carter, the governor of the borough workhouse, but over the last few months it became clear that the unmarried girl was pregnant. Turner gave birth to a boy in the workhouse infirmary on 21 May 1879 but on the following evening, the workhouse matron found the naked body of a newborn baby boy hidden in a wooden box in the cellar of the governor's house. Lieutenant Carter confronted Turner, demanding to know if she or the baby's father (a man named Stokes) were involved in its death but she denied any knowledge. At the post-mortem, a marble was found jammed in the baby's throat, which had caused its death. On this day, Turner was well enough to be remanded at Birmingham Police Court for the murder of her child and, on 13 June, she was committed to Warwick Assizes. On 7 August, Turner pleaded guilty to the lesser charge of manslaughter and was sentenced to eighteen months' imprisonment.

3 JUNE 1901 At Victoria Law Courts on this day the coroner held an inquest on the deaths of thirty-one infants found in an undertaker's cellar at Newton Row. Thirty-three-year-old Emma Knowles, the undertaker who was charged with neglecting to bury bodies and causing a public nuisance, explained that she had not realised there were so many corpses but they were all stillborn babies which she was going to bury the next day. Evidence showed that some of the bodies had lain there since

Victoria Law Courts. (Author's collection)

September 1900 but the divisional surgeon was unable to say whether any of the children died violently so the jury returned an open verdict. It was further suggested that the law concerning the disposal of stillborn infants needed reform.

4   JUNE 1893   This day saw the death of forty-eight-year-old wire rope maker Samuel Broome at Birmingham General Hospital. The married man from Garrison Street, Bordesley, worked at Messrs J.H. Wright & Co.'s rope works where one of his duties was maintenance of the machines. On Thursday, 1 June, Broome stopped a machine to repair one of the bobbins but as he was inside the machine it suddenly restarted and Broome was caught between the cogwheels. The foreman, Richard Hartley, rushed to halt the machine but it took more men to disconnect the band and by that time Broome was dreadfully mangled around his thighs and lower body. While in the hospital, Broome told his wife that his assistant, David Norton, had turned on the band instead of switching it off but at the inquest the coroner thought it was clear that the machine had been insufficiently stopped by Broome and he was responsible for his own safety. The jury returned a verdict of accidental death but recommended the appointment of a more competent man in Norton's place.

5 JUNE 1914 Thirty-year-old park policeman William Percy Savage of Auckland Road, Sparkbrook, was on duty this Friday afternoon at Walmer Recreation Ground. At shortly before five o'clock, he brought some caramel toffee from a shop near the park as he went about his rounds. Half an hour later, he suddenly collapsed to the ground and died almost instantly. A post-mortem was performed and revealed that a food substance resembling cheese was trapped in Savage's windpipe – the sweet in his mouth had not been the cause of death after all.

6 JUNE 1884 After feeling unwell for a few days, thirteen-year-old Frank Lewis was in bed at his home in Aberdovey Place, Long Acre, Nechells, on this day, when a severe thunderstorm passed overhead. Mrs Lewis came to his room and was talking to Frank when a bright flash lit up the room and he said, 'Mother it is dark; what is the time?' before falling insensible on to his pillow. A surgeon was immediately called but Frank died in his mother's arms the next day. The post-mortem revealed a contusion above his left eye which showed that the lightning was attracted by the iron bedstead, probably after coming down the chimney, and it swept along the left side of his body and struck Frank's eye. The inquest returned a verdict of death from concussion of the brain.

7 JUNE 1868 Eighteen-year-old cousins George Cox and George Smith went to visit some friends at the Sandpits, Spring Hill, on this day where they spent the evening drinking. Returning home, they had reached Hill Street when they met an elderly man who seemed much the worse for drink and was reeling about and making drunken threats. The man followed Cox and Smith, shouting that he was 'The Champion of England' and telling the 'Brummagem Puppies' to fight him. By the time they reached St Jude's church, Cox had had enough and turned to confront the stranger. They exchanged blows until a policeman arrived and the older man ran away. It was at that point that Cox realised he was bleeding profusely from the chest. The cousins went to the Queen's Hospital where the surgeon found four deep stab wounds in George Cox's abdomen which he believed were made with a rapier-like weapon and, despite prompt treatment, Cox died the following night. The inquest jury returned a verdict of manslaughter against some person unknown.

8 JUNE 1899 After his mother was taken to Erdington Infirmary seriously ill with cancer, Joseph Bowen visited her house at No. 2 back of No. 76 Arthur Street, Bordesley, to sort out her belongings. While he was there, Joseph noticed a peculiar smell coming from the cellar. He followed the growing stench to a pile of nine parcels tied with string, one of which he undid and found a sealed soap box. Removing the lid,

he was horrified to find the body of a badly decomposed baby inside. Joseph contacted the police, who arrived at the house on this day and examined the other boxes, each of which contained the body of an infant. Joseph's mother, fifty-nine-year-old Mary Bowen, acted as a midwife for the local poor and it seems that she had taken the babies that were stillborn to place in her cellar. The children, which were in various states of decomposition, showed no evidence of foul play and, as Mary soon after succumbed to her illness, the matter was taken no further.

9 JUNE 1880 When sixteen-year-old Sarah Brown was approached by a smart middle-aged man this evening offering her employment as a charwoman near her home in Handsworth, she was assured by his good manners and smart clothes. He told her that the house was in Hamstead and Brown agreed to go with him. However, when the pair reached a lonely hovel between Great Barr and Newton Road he lured her into the building and raped her. Brown's screams attracted platelayer Thomas Oxford but, instead of going to her aid, Oxford watched the assault behind a hedge. After the attack, Oxford took Brown to the police station where it transpired that another woman was similarly outraged a few weeks before. Despite the fact that Brown and Oxford were confident they would recognise the rapist he was not apprehended.

10 JUNE 1901 Forty-two-year-old John Joyce, a labourer of no fixed abode, had been in a long-running feud with Michael Nugent. A few months before, Nugent had attacked Joyce with a bayonet and he wanted revenge. On this Saturday evening, Joyce, who had been watching the Nugent house for over three hours, knocked on the door of No. 9 Court, No. 6 House, Price Street, and demanded to see Nugent. John Nugent, Michael's father, a sixty-one-year-old bamboo worker, said his son wasn't there, whereupon Joyce tried to set the house on fire by smashing a paraffin lamp. When John Nugent ran into the court for assistance, Joyce followed him, stabbing the old man through the chest with a cobbler's knife. John Nugent died on the way to the hospital and Joyce was quickly apprehended and charged with wilful murder. At Birmingham Assizes on 31 July, John Joyce was found guilty and sentenced to death. Hanged on 22 August at Winson Green Jail, Joyce showed no contrition for his crime and, when the black flag denoting his execution had taken place was raised, there were expressions of satisfaction from the assembled crowd.

11 JUNE 1910 At just after midnight on 11 June, Mrs Taylor returned to the house in Penson Road, Winson Green, which she shared with her twenty-two-year-old son, tool maker Harry Taylor. While checking that her son was also home, she was greeted by a

scene of horror. Lying on a bed in her son's bedroom was Harry's close friend, sixteen-year-old William Charles Lawrence, dead with his throat cut. Lying on another bed was Harry, with terrible wounds to his neck and a razor nearby. Harry was taken to the workhouse infirmary where he made a full recovery. It was clear that he had attacked William but, described as 'feeble minded', Harry could not account for his actions. Tried at Birmingham Assizes on 19 July, Harry was accused of killing William. The jury found him guilty of wilful murder but recommended leniency. Harry was sentenced to death but this was later commuted to penal servitude for life.

12 JUNE 1879 On this day a coroner's jury at Birmingham Police Court returned a verdict of wilful murder against thirty-five-year-old Hannah Hinks of Freeth Street. Just over a week previous, on 4 June, curiosity had gotten the better of Hannah's eighteen-year-old daughter Ann and she decided to open a box that was kept locked in her mother's bedroom. Much to her horror, however, the box contained the skeleton of a baby, still clutching a piece of its clothing. The next day, Ann visited her cousin and, after telling him of her discovery, he went to the police who immediately searched the Hinks' house. The police discovered that the box actually contained two skeletonised infants who, according to medical evidence, were born alive and killed by suffocation. Hannah was arrested and she admitted giving birth to the children but said they were born dead. Evidence was given at court by neighbours that Mrs Hinks seemed pregnant five years ago and letters were found indicating an improper intimacy with a Birmingham gentleman. Hannah was tried at Warwick Assizes in August where she pleaded guilty to the lesser charge of concealment of a birth and was sentenced to nine months' imprisonment.

13 **JUNE** 1850   On the evening of 11 June 1850,
twenty-one-year-old assistant draper Thomas
Carrington and several work colleagues decided to go
bathing in the old Birmingham Canal near Monument Lane. Only
one of the men could swim so he checked the bottom of the canal in
various places and advised his friends where they could have potential problems.
Unfortunately, Thomas, in diving from the side, was carried beyond his depth.
The only person in the group who could swim panicked and did not go to Thomas'
aid so Mr Carrington sank beneath the surface. Fifteen minutes lapsed before Thomas
was pulled from the water and though resuscitation was attempted, he could not be
saved. The inquest jury returned a verdict of accidental death.

14 **JUNE** 1894   In 1893, fifty-seven-year-old sawyer's labourer Joshua Walker
was certified insane and removed to Winson Green Asylum. Once there he showed
increasing signs of paranoia but on 16 May 1894 he was discharged, having
apparently regained his reason. Joshua went to live with his wife, sixty-year-old Emma,
and his son's family at No. 6 Court, No. 2 House, Holt Street, where he seemed happy.
However, in June, Joshua began complaining of hallucinations, pains in the head and
accusing his wife of infidelity (claims she strongly denied). Joshua and Emma went
to bed on the night of 13 June, sharing their bedroom with two granddaughters,
Florence and Emma. At about four o'clock on this morning, young Emma awoke to
find Joshua stabbing his wife repeatedly with a double-bladed knife; she ran to her
parents' room who tried to stop Joshua but he threatened them and ran into the
street. Joshua was arrested covered in blood and wandering aimlessly around the
city, the knife still in his possession. Emma was beyond help; there were twelve stab
wounds to the head, her jugular vein was severed, her tongue was nearly detached
and both thumbs were almost cut off. Brought before Birmingham Assizes on 31 July
for the wilful murder of Emma Walker, Joshua was found not responsible for his
actions and Justice Wills ordered him to be detained at Her Majesty's pleasure.

15 **JUNE** 1858   Twenty-year-old clerk Thomas Kelly and his thirteen-year-old brother
Martin were digging in the garden at their home in St James' Street, Vauxhall Road,
when their uncle suggested they go into Birmingham to see the queen, who was
visiting the city on this day. As they were dirty the two boys went to the canal near
Saltley to bathe and Martin jumped in, swimming straight across. Unfortunately,
halfway across the canal, Thomas suddenly seemed to get cramp. Martin, seeing that
his brother was starting to sink, turned back and grabbed Thomas in an attempt to

pull him to safety. However, with Thomas' weight pulling him under, Martin was forced to let go and Thomas started to sink again. By the time Martin was able to get help Thomas had drowned. At the inquest the jury returned a verdict of accidental death and sympathised with the parents on the loss of such a fine young man.

16 JUNE 1885 At Aston Police Court on this day, provision dealer John Andrews of Barton Street was charged with assaulting his child. At about half past three in the afternoon on 15 June, John came home the worse for drink. His children met him in the street and he chased them home, overtaking his two-year-old daughter Ann. When he was close behind Ann he struck her, knocking her down on to the doorstep. Ann's forehead was bleeding badly so a kind neighbour took her to the chemist to get the wound dressed but John followed them, snatching his daughter from the woman's arms and refusing to allow any treatment. A passer-by was so indignant at Andrew's behaviour that he 'pitched' into him and gave John a black eye. Fortunately for John, the witnesses failed to appear at the trial and he was acquitted.

17 JUNE 1862 The Ince family of Heneage Street were struggling to survive on the meagre wages supplied by forty-four-year-old tailoress Eleanor Ince as her husband Frederick spent much of his wages on drink. In the previous twelve months, Fredcrick had given his wife only 10s and, when intoxicated, often beat her with a poker. On this Tuesday evening, Frederick was so drunk that Eleanor was frightened to let him in the house. Forcing his way in, Frederick pushed the mother of his eight children into the fireplace. Then, when Eleanor tried to protect herself with the poker, he wrestled it from her and beat her across the face and body. One of their daughters tried to help Eleanor but Frederick also struck her and bit her hand. At Birmingham Police Court in front of Mr Kynnersley, forty-five-year-old Frederick was charged with assaulting his wife; it was the third time he had been brought before the court on a similar offence. Mr Kynnersley, after expressing a wish that the law could advocate giving wife-beaters a sound thrashing, committed Frederick to the House of Correction for six months with hard labour.

18 JUNE 1870 When nineteen-year-old blacksmith John Eagan met Mary Anne O'Neil, he was determined to become better acquainted. On this Saturday night, he followed the girl to her lodgings in No. 11 Court, No. 3 House, Edgbaston Street, and pestered her to walk out with him. Mary Anne resisted John's advances, however, and, losing his temper, he began throwing brick ends at the house. Another lodger, fifty-eight-year-old Bernard Garrity, was disturbed by the argument and rushed into

the street where a flying brick caught him on the head and fractured his skull. Bernard was taken to the Queen's Hospital, where the operation of trepanning was performed, but inflammation of the brain occurred and he died of his injuries a few days later. John was arrested and tried at Warwick Assizes on 20 July for wilful murder. He was found guilty of manslaughter and sentenced to ten years' penal servitude. On hearing the sentence, John's mother created a scene in court while John was borne shrieking from the dock.

19 JUNE 1839 A group of girls, including seventeen-year-old screw maker Mary Attwood, decided to attend the Chartist meeting being held at the Bull Ring this Wednesday evening. While they were standing by the Market Hall, an acquaintance – nineteen-year-old William Lowe – came up to the girls and began an argument with Mary, accusing her of calling him a thief. William was heard to say, 'You b___y b___r, I'll break the bridge of your b__y nose,' whereupon Mary threaded to attack William's 'Moll' or girlfriend. At that Lowe lost his temper, pushed Mary against a lamp post

The Bull Ring, 1880s. (Author's collection)

and struck her around the head and neck several times. Mary collapsed to the floor and died moments later. Members of the crowd grabbed William to prevent his escape and, when the post-mortem revealed bleeding on the brain consistent with the blows Mary received, he was charged with feloniously killing and slaying the young girl. Tried at Warwick Assizes on 29 July, William Lowe pleaded guilty but it was felt that the provocation he had received warranted a sentence of only three months' imprisonment with hard labour.

20   JUNE 1885 On Easter Monday 1885, an illegitimate baby boy, Charles Stewart Churchman, was born in Bath Row and, along with his penniless mother, was taken in by Mrs Warden of Pershore Road. Other lodgers objected to the baby, however, so Charles was sent to be nursed by a Mrs Owen of Hurst Street. Three weeks later, his mother paid a visit and was horrified to see her son in an emaciated condition. Although he was immediately removed from Mrs Owen's care, the baby's health steadily worsened and he died on 20 June, weighing just 3lbs 7oz. At the inquest on 22 June, witnesses came forward to testify that Mrs Owen was of intemperate habits and she had been seen completely drunk with baby Charles dirty and almost naked on the floor. Mrs Owen, however, felt she was being labelled unfairly: 'I wouldn't starve a cat, much less a baby ... am I to be put down as a drunkard and a murderer because I had a pint of beer?' The coroner, in summing up, pointed out that though Charles had died by starvation it did not follow he was wilfully deprived of food and evidence was not clear if anyone was criminally guilty. The jury returned a verdict of 'wilful neglect and from the want of proper nourishment and they consider Mrs Owen is a little to blame in the matter'. The coroner recorded the verdict and censured Mrs Owen for her conduct.

21   JUNE 1891 The relationship between twenty-nine-year-old publican William Hans Ringland and his twenty-five-year-old wife Matilda was extremely volatile, and on 2 June, he had been bound over to keep the peace. After spending the day out together, the couple returned to their home at The Grand Turk in St Luke's Road but at about eleven o'clock in the evening, William began swearing at Matilda. The argument escalated and William struck her across the face while she was holding their baby son. Then, when a witness got in the way, William began pelting his wife with crockery. Brought before Birmingham Police Court on 26 June for assault, William told the magistrates they could do what they liked about it and they could send him away if they chose. William Ringland was sentenced to three months' hard labour with a separation order being granted.

22 JUNE 1876 No one could doubt the affection twenty-four-year-old John Ball had for his eight-month-old son James. However, the family of three were in extremely striated circumstances since John had lost his job and, as a result, they shared their one room and bed with a lodger. John, a former steel-toy forger, was known for his melancholic disposition and it seems he began to imagine that his wife was having an affair with the lodger. At ten o'clock this morning, John was seen lovingly carrying his son from their home in Pritchard Street, Aston, but two hours later he called at a neighbour's and told them he had drowned the baby so his wife 'could have her fling' and that the only reason he hadn't killed himself was so he could tell them where James was. Concerned friends rushed to the canal near Salford Bridge where the lock keeper pulled out the body of little James, two rocks attached by a cord around his waist. A distressed John fell to the floor; 'Oh my dear lamb! Do father let me drown myself.' Taken into custody, John was removed to Warwick Gaol but his increasingly irrational behaviour meant that, at his eventual trial at Warwick Assizes in December 1876, John was declared insane and ordered to be detained during Her Majesty's pleasure. The prisoner sat on a chair with his face in his hands, apparently overwhelmed with grief.

23 JUNE 1894 When the public houses closed this Saturday night, twenty-five-year-old brass polisher Joseph Robinson of No. 4 Bow Street, Horse Fair, met his paramour Sarah Watkins and they stood chatting together near his home. While they were there, known prostitute, twenty-three-year-old Emma Collins, came up to the couple and drunkenly made several rude remarks to Joseph before pulling at Sarah's dress: 'Don't think I want your chap. When I want a chap it's one with plenty of brass.' Joseph and Sarah told Emma to go but she became more abusive until Joseph, who was rather drunk and known for his violent character, ran at Emma, hit her in the face with his fist and then kicked her twice in the stomach as she lay on the floor. The many witnesses on the street made no attempt to stop the attack or help Emma, as it was a common occurrence in the area. It was not until two police officers found her lying unconscious on the ground that an ambulance was called; by then it was too late and Emma died on the way to the Queen's Hospital. Joseph was arrested and charged with manslaughter but the post-mortem revealed that Emma died from bleeding in the brain that may not have been caused by Joseph and the case was dropped.

24 JUNE 1883 Shortly after two o'clock this Sunday morning, Inspector Evans of the Handsworth Constabulary was called to the Great Western Inn where he found thirty-one-year-old Joseph Fisher of Winson Green Road lying in a serious condition with a bullet wound to the face. Rushed to the Queen's Hospital, Fisher's prognosis

was poor when it was found that the bullet had entered the left side of the nose, travelled around the eye and lodged itself in his forehead. According to twenty-eight-year-old George Louis Zellier, the landlord of the inn, he had invited Fisher and a friend to play cards but an argument broke out when Fisher accused Zellier of not paying his debts. Fisher had left the inn but returned and a frightened Zellier threatened him with a gun. 'You could not do it if you were to try,' taunted Fisher, at which Zellier, in an excited state, pulled the trigger. However, when Fisher recovered, West Bromwich Police Court discharged Zellier, the Bench considering he was guilty of gross carelessness but not malicious intent.

25 JUNE 1839 On the morning of 7 June 1839, Edward Davis was digging out a foundation for a building on Birmingham Heath when there was a sudden collapse of earth and rubble, burying his legs before he could escape. When workmen dug Edward out it was clear that his left leg was badly damaged, with sections of bone sticking through his skin. He was conveyed to hospital but the leg became severely infected and Edward died some weeks later. The coroner's jury on this day returned a verdict of accidental death.

26 JUNE 1894 At Birmingham Police Court on this day, eighteen-year-old single mother Rose Morris was charged with neglecting her six-month-old son Henry Morris in such a way as to cause unnecessary suffering. The court heard that Henry, who was weakly, emaciated and in a filthy condition, was often left alone for several hours at their lodgings in Clyde Street, Bordesley while Rose went drinking. Witnesses said that Rose was often drunk and incapable of looking after her son. Mr Lowe, who prosecuted on behalf of the Society for the Prevention of Cruelty to Children, stated that Henry was found covered in vermin, with little clothing and open sores on his stomach and legs. Rose was found guilty and sentenced to a month in gaol with hard labour.

27 JUNE 1874 On this day, thirty-five-year-old chemist John Joseph Horton of Stratford Road was charged with raping eighteen-year-old Helen Heath. On 23 June, Helen visited John's shop where she asked for half an ounce of citrate of magnesia. John asked if the medicine was for her and if so he could give her something that would be even better. Helen agreed to take a drink of a liquid that John offered her and almost instantly she became stupefied; John then dragged her though to a back room and raped her. Helen found it impossible to call out or scream to her young man, Henry Cressell, who was waiting outside the shop. After the attack, John warned Helen to say nothing 'for her own sake' but she felt so ill that Henry made her visit a doctor on the

way home who felt she was suffering from hysteria. Although Helen did not tell the doctor or Henry about the assault, when she arrived at her home in Liverpool Lane she immediately told her mother who informed the police. However, at the Birmingham Police Court three days later, John brought forward witnesses who said that the chemist had not seen Helen at the time in question and the examining doctor told the court there was no sign of violence on Miss Heath's body. The Bench felt the accusation was 'trumped up' and, among boos and hisses, John Horton was released.

28 JUNE 1891 Late on the evening of 26 June, a midden owned by the canal company and adjoining wheelwright Charles Scutt's house in Lichfield Road, Aston, was finally emptied after two years of usage. Effluent and decayed matter was released and an offensive smell pervaded the area. By early this Sunday morning the entire Scutt family were unwell, suffering from sickness and diarrhoea, with two-year-old Mary Jane particularly ill. Sadly, after a day of violent sickness and purging, Mary Jane died. At the inquest, doctor Lumby gave cause of death as diarrhoea caused by malarial poison, which he believed came from the midden. The jury returned a verdict in accordance with medical evidence and added the rider that the canal company ought to have the midden emptied more frequently.

29 JUNE 1868 The employees of Messrs Kynoch's percussion cap factory in Witton Lane, Aston, knew how dangerous some of the manufacture processes were and indeed the mixing department was placed some 30yds from the main building. Forty-seven-year-old George Southby's job was to wet some of the fulminate compound (the powder composition of the cartridge) and he was working in the mixing shed this Monday afternoon when carpenter William Meredith came and stood by the door. William began questioning George, and it is believed this distracted the married father of five, as he shook the compound too vigorously when pouring it into a bowl. The fulminate ignited, blowing off the roof of the shed and throwing George across the room with his head severed and his stomach ripped open.

30 JUNE 1839 Twenty-year-old William Kite, a labourer upon the Birmingham and Gloucester Railway, spent Saturday evening drinking at a house of ill repute in Smithfield Passage. When he became abusive to owner Emma Hill, he was thrown out by Emma's paramour, William Lockett, at four o'clock this Sunday morning. Kite was heavily intoxicated and he fell into the lane, where Lockett proceeded to kick him in the back. Witnesses noticed Kite was ill and conveyed him to a surgeon in Digbeth but he died on the way. Lockett was arrested for murder but the post-mortem showed that Kite had died as a result of a brain injury and, as no one came forward testifying that Lockett had struck Kite around the head, he was released. The inquest returned a verdict of wilful murder on William Kite by some person or persons unknown.

JULY

1 JULY 1887 At Birmingham Quarter Sessions on this day, forty-five-year-old labourer David James of Richard Street was indicted for unlawfully wounding Ann Southall and PC Beams. On 17 June 1887, David was quarrelling with his wife when neighbour Ann tried to intervene. Angry at the intrusion, David picked up a chopper and hit Ann over the head with it, remarking, 'If you're going to fetch a copper I'll give you something to fetch him for.' As Ann fell to the floor with serious head injuries, witnesses of the attack summoned PC Beams who tried to arrest David, but he too was attacked with the chopper and soon lay badly injured on the floor. David James went to strike PC Beams again but a neighbour threw a brick and knocked James down. He was arrested while Ann and the policeman were taken to the General Hospital where, despite their injuries, they made a full recovering. At his trial, James said his wife and Ann were drunk and this had maddened him, but he had not struck Ann with the sharp end of the chopper nor attacked the police until hit first. The jury found him guilty of the charge and James was sentenced to eighteen months' hard labour.

2 JULY 1868 Eleven-week-old Henry Davies from Icknield Street East, was suffering from a cold, and so on 1 July his mother decided to use a powder she had procured for herself when she was ill. Unfortunately, the medicine contained a large amount of opium, which quickly caused young Henry to lose consciousness and fall into a coma. Medical aid was obtained but the overdose was too great and the baby died on this Thursday morning. The inquest jury considered that his mother had acted with the best intention and acquitted her of blame, returning a verdict of homicide by misadventure.

3 JULY 1878 Harriet Baker worked as a servant in the employment of pawnbroker Mr Walton of Park Lane, Aston. On this Wednesday evening, twenty-three-year-old carpenter Jason Thomas Meyler was working at the house when he realised that he was alone with Harriet. The married father of one followed her into the kitchen, grabbed her from behind and tried to rape her. Harriet reported the attack and Meyler was arrested and tried at Warwick Assizes on 8 August for attempted rape. The jury found Meyler guilty but his sentence was deferred.

4 JULY 1881 At Birmingham Police Court on this day, twenty-one-year-old glassblower Thomas Harper of Essington Street and twenty-five-year-old labourer Nelson Lydard were charged with violently assaulting three police officers. On the evening of 2 July, Harper walked up to PC White, who was on duty in Sheepcote Street, and began using aggressive and abusive language. White attempted to arrest Harper but the glassblower struck the policeman around the head and body until White lost consciousness.

PC White fell to the floor, whereupon Harper stole his staff and whistle before commencing to kick him in the head; a passer-by who tried to protect the injured officer was also assaulted. PC Battery and PC Cuff arrived and were only able to arrest Harper after several minutes of violent altercation. As the officers were taking Harper away, however, Lydard began attacking them in an attempt to rescue his friend. The court said that the assaults were of the most serious nature and sentenced Harper to four months' hard labour and Lydard to two months in gaol.

5 JULY 1890 Witnesses reported hearing cries of 'murder' coming from the home of William and Emily Ryland of Great Francis Street, Duddeston, early this Saturday morning. Neighbours entering the house found fifty-nine-year-old Emily lying on the floor, bleeding from a severe head wound and accusing her husband of stabbing her with a kitchen knife. Emily was taken to the General Hospital while fifty-year-old stamper William was arrested on the charge of unlawful wounding, a clasp knife in his pocket. William said that his wife was crazed after falling downstairs and cutting her head; he had left her lying in a pool of blood. When asked if had helped her up, William replied, 'No ___ fear.' Emily died of her wounds later that day but medical evidence showed that the death was due to exhaustion caused by an acute attack of mania not the wounds on Emily's head. William was discharged due to the medical findings and lack of any evidence that showed he inflicted the injuries; the inquest jury returned a verdict of death from exhaustion on Emily.

Birmingham General Hospital, 1809. (Author's collection)

6   JULY **1908** On Friday, 3 July, sixty-one-year-old window cleaner John Jarvis of Jenner Street was standing on a ladder in the Bull Ring carrying out a job when a blind man came down the street. Although the blind man was making plenty of noise to alert passers-by, John was deaf and didn't notice him. The blind man, unaware of the presence of the ladder, walked into it and John was thrown to the ground, a distance of over 15ft, where he landed on his head. John was taken to hospital suffering from concussion and a broken arm but he died on this day without regaining consciousness; a verdict of accidental death was returned.

7   JULY **1917** Ada Copestick lost her husband when he was killed in France in 1916. Heartbroken, she clung to her son, fourteen-year-old Edward, for comfort. On this Saturday afternoon, Edward was riding his bicycle down Great Lister Street when, suddenly finding himself between a tram and a lorry, he faltered and fell off his bike. The young lad from No. 3 Malvern Place, Coleman Street, was thrown underneath the lorry and the wheels passed over his body, killing him instantly. No blame was attributed to the lorry or tram drivers and the inquest returned a verdict of accidental death on Edward, expressing sympathy for his distraught widowed mother.

8 JULY 1865 We will probably never know for what reason forty-two-year-old Joseph Lowe beat Thomas Willis' son on this day, but it was to lead to tragic consequences. In the days that followed, Joseph – a handcuff maker living in Booth Street, Handsworth – was initially confronted by Thomas' wife Louisa, who threw stones at his back and threatened to dash his brains out. When Joseph said he would put Louisa in some water, she called her husband who challenged Joseph to a fight. The two men rolled up their sleeves and began scrapping in the street, watched by many of their neighbours. Forty-six-year-old Thomas quickly gained the upper hand and threw Joseph to the floor several times, until eventually Joseph lay defeated. Joseph was helped into his bedroom by his wife Ellen, but a couple of hours later she came screaming to neighbours that Joseph could not be roused and was turning black. A surgeon was sent for but Joseph died before he arrived. Thomas Willis was arrested and tired for manslaughter at Staffordshire Assizes on 25 July. The medical evidence decided that Joseph Lowe probably died of excitement so the jury returned a not guilty verdict and Thomas walked free.

9 JULY 1875 This day saw the trial at Warwick Assizes of twenty-year-old Jeremiah Corkery for the wilful murder of Police Constable Lines. On 5 March 1875 a burglary was committed at the Bull's Head public house in Fordrough Street by Billy Downes, who two days later was spotted in the same pub. Two policemen, Fletcher and Goodman, came to arrest Downes but, as they attempted to take him to the police station, they were followed by a large gang of men who began throwing stones in order to free Downes. As the group reached Navigation Street they met thirty-year-old PC William Lines who immediately came to his colleagues' assistance. The mob became more violent and, when Police Sergeant Fletcher was knocked to the ground, PC Lines struck the attacker. At that, Corkery drew a knife and stabbed Lines in the ear, severing his carotid artery so that blood spurted across the street. Lines was taken to the Queen's Hospital where they initially controlled the bleeding but, when an aneurism formed and pus began seeping from the wound, William deteriorated, dying on 24 March. Corkery was found guilty of the murder and sentenced to death by Justice Field. Despite hopes of a reprieve, he was executed in a private hanging at Warwick County Gaol on 27 July.

10 JULY 1865 At about nine o'clock on this Monday morning, twenty-month-old Rhoda Sarah Allen was in the kitchen of her home in No. 13 Court, No. 7 House, High Street. While her mother Sarah was distracted, little Rhoda succeeded in climbing the stool near the fire and attempted to stand on top of it. However, she lost her balance and fell forward, grabbing at a teapot of boiling hot water in an attempt to save herself. The contents tipped out, covering the child with scalding liquid and, although she was immediately wrapped up and taken to the General Hospital, she never rallied, dying from her injuries the following Tuesday evening. The inquest jury returned a verdict of accidental death.

11 **JULY 1891** On this Saturday morning, ten-year-old William Albert Ball was left to look after his two younger brothers at their home at No. 20 Pritchett Street, Aston. The three boys decided to play at 'hanging' and William attached a rope around his neck, knotted the other end to an iron bar in the mantelpiece and stood on the fender. Tragically, William's feet slipped from the fender and he was left dangling unable to touch the floor. His brothers, Edwin and Ernest, rushed to a neighbour but it was too late – William was already dead. The inquest returned a verdict of accidental death.

12 **JULY 1878** An inquest was held on this day on the death of fifty-six-year-old widow Caroline Bradbury. On 9 July, Caroline and two young ladies were passengers in a pony and trap being driven by groom Thomas Thomson. The group were returning from Birmingham and passing through Hall Green when they met two bicyclists coming along the road in the opposite direction. The pony kicked out and then bolted away before smashing the trap against a gate pillar, throwing all the occupants to the ground. Although the others escaped serious injury, Mrs Bradbury landed on her head, breaking her neck and dying instantly. The jury returned a verdict of accidental death after questioning whether there should be some legislation on bicycles' road use.

13 **JULY 1866** James David Davis decided to visit the public house next door to his home in Henry Street this Friday evening. While James was there, Thomas Taylor drank some of his beer and, when James remonstrated, Thomas attempted to hit him. James left the public house and went home but shortly afterwards Thomas entered the house and savagely attacked James until he was unconscious. Picking up a poker, Thomas then began smashing the Davis' belongings and, when James' wife Ann tried to prevent him, he attacked her too. Police officers arrived at the house and arrested Thomas, but not before he punched and kicked several officers. Tried at Birmingham Police Court for violent assault, Thomas was imprisoned for four months.

14 JULY 1868 On the evening of 14 July 1868, the dead body of a man was found lying on the Pershore Road and, although there were no marks of violence upon him, his clothing had clearly been rifled though. The body was conveyed to the Queen's Hospital where it was identified as twenty-four-year-old wood turner George Tullet of Kent Street, who had not returned home after going for a walk with neighbour William Rogers. At the inquest, Rogers said that he had left his friend at Calthorpe Park complaining of feeling low and when the post-mortem revealed prussic acid in Tullet's stomach a verdict of suicide was returned. However, in May 1869, Bernard Gallagher made a statement to the police, claiming that Rogers had confessed to killing Tullet and that he also said, 'there is another or two of the family that I mean to serve in the same way'. Sixty-two-year-old Rogers was swiftly arrested but denied having made such a statement. A cousin of Tullet's came forward saying that Rogers had threatened to poison her when she refused his advances but the police could find no evidence to connect William Rogers to the death and he was discharged.

15 JULY 1864 James Robinson lived with his mother, forty-two-year-old Elizabeth, and her second husband, thirty-three-year-old Francis Baxter, at Providence Place, Cheapside. Francis was out of work so, on this Friday morning, Elizabeth gave him some money to buy currants, which the family would use to sell on. However, when Francis returned drunk without the currants, Elizabeth demanded the money back. The couple began to fight and Francis picked up the fire shovel, striking his wife over the head with two savage blows from the iron handle before hitting her across the mouth and knocking out six teeth. James jumped to his mother's defence and was also struck across the forehead. Neighbours then intervened and a doctor was called, who arrived to find Elizabeth bleeding from the head, the teeth on the left side of her mouth broken at the gums and bruises covering her body. Elizabeth received treatment but never recovered from her injuries, dying on 28 August. Francis was tried for manslaughter at Warwick Assizes on 2 March 1865, where the jury found him guilty. Nevertheless, the judge felt that, although it was a most cowardly thing to strike a woman, he did not believe Francis intended to kill his wife, and so sentenced Francis to twelve months' imprisonment.

16 JULY 1867 Cashier James Scott had been working for Messrs Redman and Pryse, gun manufacturers of Aston Street, for several years. However, the twenty-two year old had been spending far more than he earned and was stealing money from the firm by tampering with the accounts. The discrepancies come to the notice of forty-year-old branch manager John Pryse and he appraised partner Mr Redman who, on the evening of 6 April, accused Scott of stealing. Mr Redman made it known to Scott that it was John Pryse who had discovered the stealing before sending him for the accounts book. Scott left the office and went to the gun department, where he picked up a seven-barrelled revolver, entered John's office and shot him. John's brother, Charles Pryse, heard the gunshot and rushed in to see Scott shoot John for a second time. As John fell to the floor, Charles wrestled for the pistol, which he eventually grabbed but not before being shot through the hand. Charles struck Scott across the head with the weapon, knocking him unconscious. The police arrived; Scott was taken into custody and then conveyed to the General Hospital. Sadly, John's wounds proved to be fatal so Scott was charged with wilful murder and tried at Warwick Assizes on Tuesday, 16 July. The evidence against James Scott was overwhelming and he was quickly found guilty and sentenced to death; it was therefore a surprise to many that he was later reprieved and given life imprisonment instead.

17 JULY 1865 Holder's Concert Hall was showing a ballet entitled the 'Feast of Roses', which at one point included around forty young ballerinas dancing around the principal performer, twenty-nine-year-old Mary Ann Egerton. At about ten o'clock on 3 July 1865, the girls had arranged themselves in a semi-circle on stage when fourteen-year-old Fanny Meek stood too close to the front of the stage where a naked flame had been placed. Fanny's costume, which she had added extra netting to so she could stand out among her compatriots, immediately caught fire and the young girl was enveloped in flames. Mary Ann rushed to the girl to douse the fire but her dress also began burning and the two dancers had to be wrapped in damp towels to put out the flames. Fanny was taken to the General Hospital with extensive burns on her chest, arms, calf and inside thighs. She initially rallied but symptoms of tetanus appeared and she died three days later. Mary Ann's burns seemed superficial and so she was conveyed to her home in Howe Street and her wounds were dressed. Sadly, the married mother of two became feverish and succumbed to her injuries on this Monday afternoon. At the coroner's inquest it was decided that the concert hall had taken every reasonable precaution and a verdict of accidental death was returned on the two dancers. In 1880, Mary Ann's husband, Henry, was to die in the Theatre Royal fire, Dublin.

18 JULY 1883 James George Howle was known for his 'excitable temper' and an unsteadiness of character, which was inherited, or so it was believed, from his father who was in a psychiatric hospital. The forty-three-year-old clerk had been depressed for several days when he left his home in Nechells on this Wednesday afternoon saying he was going to work. However, at eleven o'clock at night, James' body was found

lying on the down line of the railway near Acock's Green Station terribly mutilated; both his legs were cut off, his hand was torn from his arm and his skull was crushed. The doctor at the inquest believed that the head injury would have caused instant death and the jury found that Mr Howle was killed on the railway but there was no evidence as to how or why.

19 JULY 1885 When twenty-two-year-old Fanny Chapman from Essex was employed as a lady's maid by sixty-year-old James Ovens, she had no concerns over the appointment. On this Sunday evening, Fanny travelled up to Birmingham where she was met by James and continued to his house at Devonshire Villa, Gravelly Hill. However, when they got to the house, Fanny found it empty. She asked where the wife and servants were but James locked the door, forced brandy down her throat, stole her clothes and then raped her. According to Fanny, James refused to give her clothing and kept her locked up, raping her at regular intervals until she convinced a neighbour to send a letter home. James allowed Fanny to leave on 22 August but, when she reported her ordeal, he charged her with making false claims after he had dismissed her for theft. James was arrested and tried for criminal assault at Warwick Assizes in November, where letters were produced that Fanny had written saying she was happy in his employment. Despite Fanny telling the jury that she had been forced to write the letters, James was found not guilty and the case was closed.

20 JULY 1872 The alterations for the Birmingham and West Suburban Railway were taking much longer than expected and this had also affected the traffic on the Worcester Canal. The night soil collected from a large area was deposited on the Corporation Wharf; usually this was taken away by boat each night to Selly Oak Valley for manure but over the last four weeks an immense quantity had accumulated. When the canal again opened for traffic, the borough surveyor had been endeavouring (particularly due to the hot weather) to send the material away as quickly as possible and by this Saturday evening several boats were already dispatched. At about six o'clock, thirty-eight-year-old John Underhill, George Jakeman, thirty-three-year-old John Payne and his eleven-year-old son (also called John) were excavating the soil from the bottom of the 17ft-high pile when approximately 10 tons of soil slid from the top. George Jakeman narrowly escaped being covered, but the others were not so fortunate and were completely buried. Underhill was quickly discovered suffering from a broken leg but John Payne and his son were dead, suffocated by the night soil. No blame was attached to any individual and, after expressing sympathy to Payne's wife and remaining two children, the jury returned a verdict of accidental death.

21 JULY 1930 The draper's firm, Messrs William Taylor of Aston, employed sixty-four-year-old William Thomas Andrews as a bank messenger. On this Friday afternoon, Andrews was carrying approximately £900 in a bag in Aston when a car driven by twenty-one-year-old Herbert Charles Ridley pulled up beside him. Passenger Victor Edward Betts, who was also twenty-one years old, got out of the car, hit Andrews over the head with his fist and then drove away with the money. William Andrews was rushed to Birmingham General Hospital but died without regaining consciousness three days later. Ridley and Betts, meanwhile, went to Portsmouth, Leeds and Brighton where they spent large amounts of money. The pair were caught when they crashed a car into a ditch and needed hospital treatment. They were charged with the wilful murder of Andrews and tried at Birmingham Assizes on 5 December. The defence argued that the robbers had not intended to kill Andrews but the jury found the pair guilty and they were sentenced to death. Betts was executed at Winson Green Prison on 3 January 1931 but Ridley's sentence was commuted to life imprisonment. After serving just five years, Ridley was released on licence in 1935 and was repeatedly in court on charges of burglary.

22 JULY 1924 On the evening of 5 June 1924 the body of a baby boy was found in a kit-bag in the cloakroom at New Street Station. Evidence discovered in the bag led the police to twenty-one-year-old Charles Welford Travis, an American who was living with

The Old Bailey.

his wife, Myra, in Marylebone, London. When questioned, Charles admitted that the child was his ten-month-old son, Welford Dean Travis. At about one o'clock that morning, Charles had been woken by his son, who was teething, and, in order to stop the cries, he had placed his hand over Welford's mouth. When he removed his hand, he realised that the baby was no longer breathing, so he woke his wife and told her their son had died. She immediately said they should call a doctor but Charles felt the death looked suspicious and convinced her that they should hide the body. Taking a morning train to Birmingham, Charles dumped the child and returned to London where he made preparations to travel to America. Tried at the Old Bailey on this day, Charles was found guilty of manslaughter and sentenced to five years' imprisonment.

23 **JULY** **1879** This day saw the inquest into the death of forty-year-old labourer Joseph Holt of Mushroom Green, Dudley. On 18 July, Holt and fellow worker Richard Small were engaged in boring a hole for blasting at the building of the new asylum buildings on Rubery Hill. Once the hole was made, the two men should have informed the 'firer' who would set the charge, but they decided to collect the gunpowder from the powder magazine and charge it themselves. Using a steel rod from the boring, the two men began ramming the powder into the hole when there was a sudden explosion as the gunpowder ignited. Holt's face took the force of the blast, shattering his skull and destroying his eyes while Small was also badly injured. The two labourers were taken to the Queen's Hospital but Holt died four days later. At the inquest the foreman told the coroner that Holt and Small had only been working for them for nine days and would not have been allowed to set or fire the charge. The jury returned a verdict of accidental death but advised that gunpowder should be kept out of the reach of everyone but the charger.

24 **JULY** **1865** At ten o'clock on the evening of 16 July, neighbours saw twenty-two-year-old John Moran viciously attacking his twenty-one-year-old partner Bridget Coyne in Thomas Street. John smashed something into Bridget's face, knocked her down and kicked her several times as she held their baby. Sadly this was a common occurrence and friends told Bridget that it was her fault for not reporting John, with whom she had been cohabiting for two years. Two days later, John attacked and robbed Bridget's father James in the street. Mere hours afterwards, Bridget was found lying in John Street, covered in blood. John was arrested for the assault on James Coyne but, when Bridget died on this day and the post-mortem revealed that a piece of tobacco pipe had been pushed into her eye where it had penetrated the brain, John was charged with her death as well. He was tried for manslaughter at Warwick Assizes but the doctor at the trial said that the fatal injury must have been caused after the altercation on the 16th and there was no evidence that John had attacked Bridget with the pipe. John escaped a verdict of manslaughter and, with insufficient evidence concerning his attack on James – as he also had an alibi – the case was dismissed.

25 **JULY** **1845** Visiting Birmingham on business, thirty-six-year-old Benjamin Myatt Harlow, a prominent brass founder from Derbyshire, was driving his gig down Constitution Hill this Friday evening. Witnesses recall seeing Harlow playing his whip along the back of his mare when she suddenly bolted. Despite his attempts to stop the mare, the gig careered to Snow Hill where it ran into a stationary omnibus. The gig was smashed to pieces and Harlow was thrown head first to the ground, where he

was dragged for several yards by the horse. Harlow's head made violent contact with the pavement and he was unconscious when conveyed to the General Hospital where he died early Saturday morning. The inquest returned a verdict of accidental death before Harlow was laid to rest in his home village of Ashbourne.

26 JULY 1860 This Thursday afternoon, thirty-nine-year-old labourer Patrick Cantlin was employed at the premises of confectioner Mr Hill at Horse Fair. Mr Hill's bricklayer had erected a new oven and Patrick was involved in cleaning the debris from the back when the arched ceiling suddenly collapsed. Patrick was buried beneath such a mass of bricks and mortar that when he was finally pulled out he was dead, shockingly crushed by the weight of the ceiling. The inquest returned a verdict of accidental death on the married father of six whose wife was five months pregnant at the time of his demise.

27 JULY 1865 Eleven-year-old William Augustus Sherwin left his home in Hatchett on this Thursday morning, ostensibly to find some employment. However, by midday the boy was bathing in the Birmingham Canal between Lancaster Street Bridge and the Aston Road Bridge, where he decided to steal some coal lying by the side of Lewis' wharf. Joseph Sillitoe, who was in charge of the wharf, caught him red-handed and rushed out, whipping at William, who evaded the blows by swimming further out. Mr Sillitoe was angered to see William laughing and pulling faces at him, so he picked up a small piece of coal and threw it at the boy, catching him on the head. It quickly became apparent that William was hurt and Mr Sillitoe took him to

the General Hospital where his wound was dressed. Young William went home and initially told his mother that he had been attacked by a man when he was playing in the water but, when he grew more ill, the true story came out. Sadly, William Sherwin died of a skull fracture and blood loss on 1 August. At the inquest no blame was attached to Joseph Sillitoe, who was said to be very distressed by the boy's death, and the jury returned a verdict of 'homicide by misadventure'.

28 JULY 1888 The Aston slogging gang prevented their members from being sent to jail by clubbing together to pay any fine imposed by the court. On this Saturday, however, the gang decided to ask bicycle maker James Russell to contribute to the fund. James, of Catherine Street Aston, had no involvement in the gang and refused to pay, whereupon gang members Alfred Simpson and George Betts struck him before kicking him and hitting him with belt buckles. James escaped to a neighbours and a police officer, who had witnessed the attack, was able to arrest Betts. Simpson was subsequently arrested and, despite promising to leave the country if the court were lenient, he was sentenced to two months' imprisonment with hard labour.

29 JULY 1892 At Birmingham Police Court on this day, Robert Hull and his wife Kate of St Andrew's Road, Small Heath, were summoned for neglecting their six children, who were aged between ten years and seven months. Inspector Thompson of the National Society for the Prevention of Cruelty to Children visited the Hull's home on 24 June and found it in a filthy condition. All of the children were in a terribly dirty state; there were sores on their heads, which were covered in vermin, and their clothes were ragged. The children's beds and bedding was filthy and lice ridden. Thompson issued Robert and Kate with a warning but, when he returned a few weeks later, there was no improvement; indeed Kate was clearly under the influence of drink. The children were examined by a doctor, who reported that one child had rickets and water on the brain, while another seemed to have no control of bodily movements. In court each parent blamed the other; Kate told the Bench that she was regularly beaten and feared Robert, while he claimed that Kate used much of their income on alcohol. The stipendiary remarked that the children were terrorised by their father and sentenced him to three months' imprisonment with hard labour. It was decided that neighbours would ensure Kate looked after the family and further checks made. By 1894, however, the Hull family were again investigated and found to be in the same disgusting state; both parents were imprisoned for several months and the five remaining children (one had died) were removed to the workhouse.

30 JULY 1839 This day saw sixty-one-year-old Luke Wilde walk free from Warwickshire Assizes when the Grand Jury found him not guilty of the murder of his wife Rose. On 8 July, at about half past seven in the morning, Rose Wilde visited publican Joseph Dudley for a glass of gin and seemed pensive about Luke's mood. Their neighbours in Mount Street were well aware of the couple's violent relationship and their frequent arguments – only the week before Rose was seen with a black eye and bruises on her body. At eight o'clock the Wildes were witnessed fighting at their home where Luke was heard calling Rose a 'bloody whore'. When the Wilde's lodger entered the kitchen at half past nine, he found Rose hanging from a cord suspended from the ceiling. Her body was quickly cut down but she was already dead. Luke, who was in bed, seemed shocked about his wife's death but it soon became clear that Rose could not have hanged herself; no chair or stool was close enough to use. Luke was arrested on the charge of wilful murder but, although the court knew Rose could not have committed suicide, there was no evidence that Luke had caused her death and they had no alternative but to release him.

31 JULY 1861 On 4 June 1861, twenty-two-year-old Henry Stryde was fixing a strap on the drum of the revolving main shaft at the Old White Lead Works, Spring Hill, when the ladder he was on slipped and Henry was pitched forward on to the moving shaft. The machinery was quickly halted but both of Henry's legs were badly damaged. Henry, of Icknield Street West, was taken to the General Hospital where his right leg was amputated. Unfortunately the left leg developed bacterial erysipelas which caused blood poisoning and Henry died today. The inquest jury returned a verdict of accidental death.

AUGUST

1 AUGUST 1888 Thirty-eight-year-old Jeremiah Darcy was brought in to the Queen's Hospital this Wednesday night complaining of neck pain. Jeremiah believed that he had swallowed a set of false teeth while asleep the night before and they had become lodged in his throat. Medical staff put him under chloroform and tried to extract the teeth using forceps but they were firmly jammed in the man's oesophagus. The doctors cut his throat open to remove the teeth but sadly Jeremiah died from acute pleurisy a few days later. The inquest found that everything had been done to save Jeremiah's life and agreed with the medical evidence given.

2 AUGUST 1865 Twenty-nine-year-old William Brown was employed by the Great Western Railway Company as an engine driver. On this Wednesday evening, William was driving a goods train from Wolverhampton to Bordesley when, as they were passing through the Birmingham tunnel, the coupling of a truck broke and seventeen of the trucks were left behind. Stopping the train at the pointsman's box near Bordesley Station, William descended from the engine and was crossing the tracks when an express passenger train appeared, travelling in the opposite direction. The buffer plank knocked William down and the train passed over him, crushing his legs and shattering his head. The inquest jury returned a verdict of accidental death.

3 AUGUST 1839 On this day, the *Birmingham Journal* reported the tragic story of Harriet Herringshaw from New John Street. Harriet had been keeping the company of saddler William Orger for three years but when she fell pregnant he deserted her and refused to have anything to do with her or the baby son subsequently born in July 1839. Harriet moved in with her married sister, Elizabeth Handley, but seemed depressed and said she 'wished she was at the bottom of the canal, baby and all'. On the evening of 27 July 1837, Harriet's sister returned to the house to find it locked and bolted with the sounds of her children inside. She forced the window and, finding her eldest child tied to a bedpost, was told that Harriet had put her there. Rushing to her sister's room, Elizabeth was horrified to discover Harriet hanging from a pole with the baby hanged beside her, both dead. The inquest jury returned a verdict of suicide while in a state of insanity. They also wished to express their opinion that the conduct of Orger had been most disgusting and disgraceful.

4 AUGUST 1858 At Warwick Assizes in December 1858, thirty-nine-year-old bookkeeper James Blakesley pleaded not guilty to threatening his cousin Zachariah Twamley with a loaded pistol and stealing over 10s from his relative. For some time Blakesley had been out of work and often demanded money and food from Twamley, a farmer living in Aston. On 4 August 1858, Twamley saw his cousin lying in the grass near his house and went over to him, offering a few shillings from his purse. Blakesley rudely refused the money but then jumped up, took out a pistol, cocked it and said, 'Now, it's you or me; I mean to have all you've got.' Realising the gun was loaded and in fear for his life, Twamley gave Blakesley his purse and he casually sauntered away. In his defence, Blakesley said he would not have shot his cousin but the jury returned a guilty verdict and the judge had no hesitation in sentencing Blakesley to five years' penal servitude.

5 AUGUST 1883 When thirty-year-old lapidary John Duke of Tower Street changed a sovereign at the General Elliot Hotel, Hill Street, this Sunday evening, he attracted the attention of known thugs twenty-one-year-old Martin McGann and nineteen-year-old William Ryan. As John left the hotel the two men attacked him from behind, threw him violently to the ground and began to rifle though his pockets. John tried to cry out but he was grabbed around the throat before being kicked around the head, fracturing his skull and knocking out several of his teeth. After McGann and Ryan ran away leaving John insensible, he was taken to the Queen's Hospital but he never regained consciousness and died on 23 August. The two men were charged with wilful murder in their absence but despite a reward of £100 for their capture and several reported sightings, McGann and Ryan were never brought to trial.

An illustration of a garotte robbery, *Illustrated Police News*, 7 August 1880. (Author's collection)

6 AUGUST 1876 Several children were playing by the canal side near Aston Road on this Sunday afternoon, including three-year-old William Upton of No. 6 Court, No. 55 Summer Lane. One of the older boys, by the name of Gould, ran across a lock and was closely followed by William who, moments later, was seen falling into the water. The lock keeper was almost immediately at the scene but it was already too late and William was dead when his body was recovered from the canal. At the inquest it emerged that Gould had told William to dive into the water, which he had done, but William's mother said he was far too timid a child to have done so. Gould's mother told the coroner that her son was a troublesome, idle lad whom she wished to get into a reformatory school, and she believed he could have pushed William in. The jury were not able to get a clear account of how the child came to be in the water but decided his death was accidental and passed the verdict accordingly.

7 AUGUST 1838 Mrs Rushton, of Lower Tower Street, was standing at her door this afternoon when she observed a young girl walking down the road. Coming in the opposite direction, she saw sixteen-year-old William Cordwell who, when he spotted the girl (later identified as Charlotte Jones), crossed the street and struck her a blow on the side of the neck which sent her reeling to the floor. 'There, d__n you, you know what it is for,' said Cordwell before walking away. Mrs Rushton and other witnesses raised the semi-conscious girl from the floor and placed her in a chair, which they lifted up to carry her to the hospital. Unfortunately one of the women holding Charlotte let go and she fell forward some 3ft to the ground. Taken to hospital, Charlotte never regained consciousness, dying within minutes. William Cordwell was arrested and an inquest was held where it transpired that he and Charlotte had had a 'slight quarrel' the night before. The post-mortem indicated that Charlotte had died from the head injury caused by falling from the chair, so although the coroner felt Cordwell was morally guilty he could not be legally guilty. The jury reluctantly returned a verdict of accidental death and Cordwell was released.

8 AUGUST 1882 Early this morning, Michael Rafferty and Charles Summerfield, after spending much of the previous night consuming large amounts of alcohol, began a drunken brawl in Cheapside. At some point the two men wrestled to the floor and, when they parted, Summerfield realised he had been stabbed in the stomach. He received treatment at the Queen's Hospital and Rafferty was charged with unlawful and malicious wounding. However, Summerfield refused to take the oath in court, claiming that he did not want to prosecute. Found guilty of contempt of court, Summerfield was sentenced to seven days in gaol at which he left the court 'tripping gaily from the witness box ... and laughing to his friends'. Rafferty, meanwhile, was sentenced to twelve months' imprisonment at the Birmingham Quarter Sessions, where he remarked, 'Thank you sir, I am satisfied. I thought there was something else coming.'

9 AUGUST 1862 Former shoemaker, thirty-two-year-old Robert Williams, had for the last eighteen months kept the Wellington Arms Tavern in New Street, Aston, with his thirty-one-year-old wife Margaret. Although he had been an accomplished cobbler, Robert and Margaret were not good innkeepers, partly because they took to drinking a lot of the stock. The couple began to fight frequently and it was not uncommon for Robert to beat his wife when drunk. At about two o'clock this Saturday morning, Robert allegedly arrived home intoxicated to find Margaret lying asleep on the floor of their bedroom and, leaving her there, he went to sleep in the children's room. However, when a servant went to wake Mrs Williams, she found her dead, her body covered in bruises. Robert, when told of the tragedy, exclaimed, 'Good God ... the cursed drink has done its work,' before rushing out of the house like a maniac. Robert evaded arrest until he was apprehended in London on 11 December, living with a Mrs Beach, who went on the run with him, leaving her husband in the process. Tried for manslaughter at Warwick Assizes on 26 March 1863, the post-mortem revealed that Mrs Williams had died of internal haemorrhaging from three broken ribs and a ruptured liver, probably caused by a violent kick. Although suspicious marks were found on Robert's boots, the jury decided there was not enough evidence and he was acquitted.

10 AUGUST 1901 Employed by London and North Western Railway as a nightwatchman, twenty-three-year-old Thomas Hibbs was aware of the dangers involved. Hibbs was working in the Curzon Street goods yard on this Saturday evening when it is believed that he saw men stealing coal. Hibbs gave chase along the canal side and a struggle ensured whereupon Hibbs was smashed over the head and thrown in the canal near Fazeley Street. The body of the young man, his skull severely fractured, was found later that night and over the next few days William Billingsley, Charles Webb and Frank Parslow were arrested after they were overheard discussing their involvement. At the initial inquiry, however, none of the men could be placed at the scene by witnesses and the three denied attacking Hibbs. The coroner pointed out that there was a lack of evidence to charge anyone for the crime and so the jury decided that Thomas Hibbs was murdered by some person or persons unknown and recommended the railway companies should have two patrols in such dangerous neighbourhoods.

11 AUGUST 1858 On 9 August 1858, William Gregory went to bed early at his home in Pershore Street due to illness. The Gregory family lived above their bonnet and haberdashery shop and, at about eleven o'clock, William was woken by cries of fire from a servant. He immediately rushed to the attic room above him, rescued his son and then tried to enter the bedroom of his daughter Eliza but was beaten back by the smoke. Leaving the house, William found neighbours raising a ladder to Eliza's window and PC Farrall was attempting to climb up. The fire brigade were also quickly on the scene but one of the firemen, Enos Edwards, took exception to Farrall ascending the ladder and trained the water on him so he could not climb. By the time Farrall was able to rescue five-year-old Eliza it was too late, the child had suffocated due to smoke inhalation. At the inquest on this day, the surgeon who performed the post-mortem felt that Eliza would have survived if rescued earlier and, as a result, the jury then returned a verdict of manslaughter against Enos Edwards. The fireman was tried at Warwick Assizes in March 1859 where he said the smoke had been so dense that he was unable to see the policeman; the jury returned a verdict of not guilty.

12 AUGUST 1876 This day saw the inquest into the death of thirty-eight-year-old Charles Porter of Digbeth. Charles worked as a surgeon in Digbeth but was well known as an alcoholic, with his wife Emma testifying that 'sometimes he would be intoxicated every day of the week'. On the evening of 10 August, Emma collected Charles from a public house so that he could make up medicine for some waiting patients. Afterwards, Charles fell into a drunken sleep on the sofa, before waking up, pouring some liquid into a glass of ginger beer and drinking it. Suddenly, an ashen-faced Charles told Emma that he thought he had drunk acid. Soon afterwards he died and, at the inquest, Emma Porter explained that her husband would often take drugs to sober himself up. The jury returned a verdict that Charles Porter had died through taking an overdose of prussic acid by misadventure.

13 AUGUST 1842 George Toy lived at his father's farm in Edgbaston where he often enjoyed shooting game, sometimes accompanied by twenty-one-year-old farm labourer John Richards. On this Saturday afternoon, George, who was lame and needed a crutch to walk, met John at the farmhouse for a drink. After a while, John left to go home and George collected his gun, setting off to do some shooting on his potato field. When George did not return for his tea, however, his concerned father sent out a search party to look for his son. At five o'clock on Sunday morning, the body of George Toy was found lying on his back in a dry ditch with his gun on his stomach. George's body was examined and it was quickly ascertained that he had been shot from behind, with the bullet entering below his right ear, at the side of his neck. The shot, which had severed both his carotid artery and jugular vein, causing instant death, had been taken from close range, judging by the singeing on George's hair. Money and a watch belonging to George were also missing. Suspicion quickly fell on John, who had been witnessed by several people walking with George around the fields and close to where the body was found. On the Saturday night, John had been seen with a watch that looked remarkably like George's and spending a surprising amount of money, especially as he only worked one day in the last fortnight. John Richards was arrested but denied seeing George that afternoon and the watch was not in his possession. While awaiting trial, John confided in his cellmate that there was no proof he had been in the area and his father had 'made all right' with the watch. At Warwick Assizes in April 1843, he was tried for wilful murder but, despite all the evidence to the contrary, the jury decided he was not guilty and John was released without charge.

14 AUGUST 1833 This Wednesday, fifty-year-old George Goodman and his wife were walking along the Worcester and Birmingham Canal, after spending the evening at the local public house, when they reached the Edgbaston tunnel which runs beneath Church Road. As they walked under the tunnel, George, who was rather intoxicated, suddenly reeled and fell into the water. Sadly before help could be obtained a boat coming along the canal ran over him, crushing his skull and killing him instantly. The coroner's inquest returned a verdict of accidental death.

15 AUGUST 1917 Six-year-old Gladys Lilian Harris of No. 5, back No. 43, Vicarage Road, Aston, was playing in the yard on 14 August when it suddenly began to rain. The children ran for shelter and several of them, including Gladys, went into the wash house where a fire was burning to heat water. In the rush to fit inside, Gladys was pushed against the fire and her dress caught fire. Despite prompt attention from neighbours and doctors, the coal carter's daughter died from her burns on this day at the General Hospital.

16 AUGUST 1882 After spending the evening drinking, fifty-two-year-old carpenter Joseph Osbourne and his wife, fifty-five-year-old Elizabeth, began arguing about money in their home at No. 39 Rea Street tonight. As the quarrel became more heated, Elizabeth ran out to the yard with a beer jug in her hand and, when Joseph followed her, threw it at him. The jug smashed at Joseph's feet and he was so incensed that he picked up one of the larger pieces and hurled it back at her, striking his wife on the forehead and inflicting a serious wound. Taken to the Queen's Hospital, Elizabeth's cut was stitched and she was allowed home but erysipelas set in and she died on the morning of 28 August. Joseph was committed to Warwick Assizes on 14 November for manslaughter, where it was revealed that Elizabeth had been an intemperate woman and Joseph clearly had no intention of killing his wife. Joseph was found guilty but, after the jury recommended mercy, he was sentenced to four years' imprisonment.

17 AUGUST 1850 On the evening of 16 June 1850, twenty-five-year-old Thomas William Green was drinking with some friends at The Sportsman public house in Garrison Lane when they began arguing with brothers Michael and James Connor. Before the situation turned violent, Thomas and his companions left but three hours later they returned to find Michael and James waiting for them outside the inn with a gang and a skirmish ensured. In the melee, James Connor threw a stone, striking Thomas on the forehead. Thomas retreated into a passage but Michael followed the injured man and smashed him over the head twice with a hammer. Rushed to the hospital, the surgeon found Thomas suffering from two serious skull fractures. A piece of bone was sticking into his brain and, despite treatment, he died on this day from inflammation on the brain. At the inquest on 17 August, Michael Connor was found guilty of manslaughter and James with aiding and abetting. They were committed to the next Warwick Assizes in March 1851 where James was acquitted but Michael was sentenced to twenty years' transportation.

18 AUGUST 1896 When ten-year-old May Lewis failed to return home after school on the Tuesday afternoon of 10 March 1896, her worried parents spent the night looking for her without success. Eventually, workmen passing a house in Vyse Street noticed the mangled body of a young girl in the front garden, and it was quickly identified as May. Police searched the building and found the rooms saturated with blood. The owners of the house were arrested but it soon came to light that only their son, twenty-three-year-old carter Frank Taylor, resided at the house. Frank was found and witnesses came forward who testified to seeing him encouraging a child into the house. The post-mortem on May revealed that she had been raped and

her skull smashed in with a brick; her body was also wet where Taylor had tried to secrete her in the attic water cistern. At his trial at Birmingham Assizes on 30 July, it emerged that Taylor had tried to drown himself on the night of the 10th but said he remembered nothing concerning May's death. The jury had no hesitation in finding Taylor guilty of wilful murder and he was privately executed on this day at Birmingham Gaol, the crowd giving vent to loud cheers as the black flag was hoisted.

19 AUGUST 1881 Forty-year-old painter Frederick Croton was in bed with his wife Emma at their home in Charles Henry Street on 17 August when they began arguing about Emma's alleged infidelity. As the quarrel escalated, Frederick left the room, only to return moments later with a carving knife. He attempted to strangle his wife before stabbing her through the arm and thigh. Although Emma was seriously hurt, she escaped further harm when her skirts stopped the knife thrusts towards her abdomen. Frederick then left the house, went to friends in Balsall Heath and told them he 'had done for her'. As Emma was taken to hospital the father of three fled but was apprehended on this day and charged with malicious violence. Frederick's defence at Birmingham Police Court on 23 August was that they were drinking heavily and it was the first time he had used a knife on his wife; he was sentenced to six months' imprisonment.

20 AUGUST 1865 At about ten past twelve this Sunday morning, Zachariah Froggatt was walking along the towpath of the Old Birmingham Canal near the Fazeley Street Bridge when he saw a boatman lying upon a woman who seemed to be struggling. When the boatman saw Froggatt he got up and walked away but the woman, whose skirts were much disordered, seemed dazed and unable to stand so Froggatt went to get help. When he returned with a policeman the woman was gone but cries of 'Oh! Let me go' could be heard from a nearby boat. Incredibly neither man investigated further but a few hours later the body of a woman was found floating in the canal. The body, identified as forty-five-year-old widow Ellen Cunningham from No. 8 Court, No. 2 House, Milk Street, was recognised by Froggatt as the missing woman and a twenty-five-year-old boatman named Joseph Blakeman was quickly apprehended as her attacker. The post-mortem revealed no evidence of violence so Blakeman was released due to insufficient evidence and a verdict of 'found dead' was returned on Cunningham.

21 AUGUST 1886 On the morning of 3 July 1886, thirty-six-year-old Sarah Taylor sent her eldest daughter, Sarah Ann, to Greets Mill Farm where her husband William was working. When the young girl returned to her home in Hall Green, Yardley, she

was met with a scene of horror. Mrs Taylor was lying in a pool of blood on the floor of the bedroom, a terrible gash across her throat and an open razor in her hand. Although she was still alive, three-year-old James Taylor and ten-month-old Herbert Taylor (two of Sarah's seven children) were on the bed, their heads almost severed from their bodies. Sarah was taken to the General Hospital where she made a full recovery but was unable to explain her actions. Tried for murder at Solihull this Saturday, Sarah was described as a delicate and odd woman somewhat prone to fits of depression. She was found guilty and committed to the assizes on the capital charge but before the trial Sarah was certified insane and removed to an asylum.

22 AUGUST 1864 This day saw the conclusion of the coroner's inquest into the death of five-month-old Edmund John Thompson. In August 1864, Edmund's unmarried mother, twenty-year-old Lucy Thompson, was forced to leave her lodging in Church Street when she could not afford to pay the rent. The unemployed bridle stitcher and her baby spent the day wandering around the city looking for work or cheaper lodgings but without success. By the evening, Lucy was desperate and hungry so she visited Edmund's father, begging for sixpence to purchase a place to sleep. As he had abandoned Lucy when she became pregnant it was no surprise when he refused, telling her to shift as best she could. With nowhere else to go, Lucy spent several nights in St Paul's churchyard. On 4 August, she went to a local chemist shop, obtained vermin powder and gave it to her baby. Immediately overcome with remorse, Lucy rushed to her brother's home but it was already too late. The post-mortem showed that Edmund had died from strychnine poisoning and Lucy was sent to Warwick Assizes on the charge of murder. Much sympathy was shown to Lucy's plight and, as it was clear she was unstable, the jury returned a verdict of not guilty on the grounds of insanity and the judge ordered her to be detained during Her Majesty's pleasure.

23 AUGUST 1889 After a month spent in hospital with a self-inflicted wound to the throat, sixty-three-year-old Charles Lister Higginbottom was well enough on this day to come before magistrates on the charge of murdering seventy-three-year-old Winifred Whittaker Phillips. On 13 July 1889, Charles, who had lodged with Winifred for the last

three years at Guilford Street, Lozells, was accused of stealing a pair of her stockings. He seemed to have resented the accusation and a quarrel took place, as the result of which he was given notice to quit his lodgings. A neighbour overheard Charles threatening to dash the old woman's head in and on the evening of 18 July, he carried out his threat; striking Winifred with a coal hammer until her skull was smashed in. Charles then attempted to commit suicide with a carving knife but medical assistance was procured and his life was saved. Magistrates passed the case on to Warwick Assizes where, unsurprisingly, Charles was found guilty of wilful murder and sentenced to death. Hanged at Warwick Gaol on 7 January 1890, Charles expressed sorrow for his crime. As his body dropped from the scaffold the rope reopened his neck wound and blood spurted from the artery all over the walls of the pit.

24 AUGUST 1840 This evening fifty-two-year-old landlady Sarah Chirm was descending Hockley Hill in a gig with her son when twenty-three-year-old servant Richard Allen came galloping past. Allen's horse struck Mrs Chirm's horse, causing the gig to overturn and throwing the occupants on to the road but Richard continued on his way. Sarah was clearly injured and when she was taken to her home at The Beehive in Handsworth, it was discovered that her right arm was fractured in several places with shards of bone clearly visible. The attending physician recommended amputation but Mrs Chirm refused. Unfortunately, infection soon set in and caused blood poisoning, killing Sarah on 27 August. Richard was arrested for the manslaughter of Sarah Chirm and tried at Staffordshire's Lent assizes in March 1841. Richard's defence was that he had not been riding fast enough to cause the accident but the jury found him guilty of Sarah's death. As Richard had already spent six months in gaol awaiting trial the judge sentenced him to one week's imprisonment.

25 AUGUST 1892 Actor Reynaud Cooper was engaged at the Grand Theatre, taking part in *The Swiss Express* with his brothers 'The Renands'. While in Birmingham, thirty-five-year-old Reynaud took lodgings at No. 21 Easy Row with his wife Rosa and children, and they seemed a happy and contented family. On the morning of 21 August, Reynaud was playing with the children in the sitting room when he noticed that a bottle containing poison used to clean buttons was sitting on the table. He asked Rosa to put it out of the reach of the children and so she put it on the mantelpiece before leaving the room. Suddenly the actor shouted for his wife. She ran into the room to find Raynaud holding the bottle, 'I have taken some ... get me some milk.' But before

anymore could be done, Raynaud fell to the floor and died. The post-mortem, held on this day, revealed that Mr Cooper had drunk a mixture of potassium and prussic acid, a virulent and rapid poison, which was used to clean metal. At the inquest it transpired that Raynaud suffered from occasional heart pains so would take some lavender water to ease the pain. The lavender water was kept on the mantelpiece and it is believed he picked up the wrong bottle while distracted by the children.

26 AUGUST 1879 Although married to jeweller Henry Vernum, twenty-five-year-old Sarah Alice Vernum began staying out all night from their home in Shakespeare Road in the company of John Ralph. Sarah and John, a twenty-eight-year-old hawker living in Winson Green, often met in various public houses around the city and, on the evening of 31 May 1879, were seen at the Why Not public house in Lodge Road. The couple left the inn and, at approximately one o'clock on Saturday morning, cries were heard coming from the canal side at Spring Hill. Shortly afterwards, John walked up to PC Burton and confessed to the murder of a women whose body could be found in the canal. A search quickly discovered the remains of Sarah, whose throat had been cut from ear to ear, and John was arrested and taken to Kenion Street Police Station. John admitted that he and Sarah had fallen out and the quarrel had quickly escalated. He was found guilty of wilful murder on 5 August at Warwick Assizes and publicly hanged at Warwick Gaol on 26 August after a final interview with his wife.

27 AUGUST 1880 Thirty-three-year-old John Caswell was employed as a machine tester at W. and T. Avery's beam and scale works, Digbeth. This Friday evening, a plate of a 5-ton road-weighing machine was being hoisted by a crane and, while Caswell was looking after the chain of the crane, the bolt which held the plate snapped. The plate fell and struck him on his left thigh, fracturing it badly. The plate edge also struck further down his leg, ripping it open down to the ankle, severing several arteries and breaking a bone. The married father of five was immediately taken to the Queen's Hospital where, despite the serious injuries, he made a full recovery.

28 AUGUST 1888 In 1884, while twenty-five-year-old Harry Benjamin Jones and George Richard Harris were working at the same factory, they struck up a friendship and Harry moved in with George and his wife Sarah. George quickly became suspicious of the intimacy between Harry and Sarah and threw Harry out. Nevertheless, the lovers continued to meet in secret until they fell out and Harry was imprisoned for three months after attacking Sarah. In February 1887, Harry

returned to Aston, where he found Sarah living alone in Sutherland Street as George was working away. According to Harry, he moved in with Sarah and her daughter, two-year-old Florence Mabel, who Harry believed was his. In early 1888, Sarah gave birth to William Harold but when George returned unexpectedly in June, Sarah threw Harry out, saying they were over. On 14 June, Harry bought a pistol, went to the Harris house and, when George and Sarah came into the yard, he was waiting with the gun. Harry shot George in the back before turning the gun on his former lover and shooting her twice in the shoulders. He then jumped through the window into the back room where Florence was playing and fired at her before striking her on the head and fracturing her skull. Rushing upstairs, Harry found baby William and struck him on the head with the butt of his gun before making his way back to where Sarah was lying and beating her violently. Witnesses eventually overpowered Harry and the Harris family were taken to the General Hospital where Florence died on 21 June. Harry was tried for wilful murder at Birmingham Assizes, where Sarah denied any affair or that either of the children were Harry's. It was no surprise that Harry Jones was found guilty and sentenced to hang at Winson Green Goal on 28 August. Harry apparently struggled for four minutes after he was hanged and his death agonies were terrible to witness.

29 AUGUST 1900 No one was quite sure what triggered forty-eight-year-old Fanny Hall's attack on her neighbour forty-six-year-old Emma Poole this Wednesday evening, but the residents of Kitchener Street were unsurprised. Taken before the Birmingham Police Court on 3 September, Mrs Hall was described as 'drunken, violent, insulting and a terror to the neighbourhood' amongst other things. The court found Fanny guilty of assault and of smashing the windows of the houses adjoining her own – she was ordered to pay 23s and costs.

30 AUGUST 1890 Sixteen-year-old Hannah Jane Sutton, who lived with her widowed mother in No. 3 House, No. 4 Court, High Street, Deritend, was known to be keeping company with twenty-year-old Hugh Royston, 'one of the biggest scamps in town'. Royston readily admitted he was Hannah's pimp but 'if she gives me sixpence a week I thought I was lucky'. On this Saturday afternoon, Hannah argued with her mother and her mother's lover James Wells who wished her to stop seeing Royston and she ran from the house. Hannah was next spotted by friend Elizabeth Walker with cuts on her head and neck. 'Oh, Lizzie, my heart's broke!' Hannah cried, 'I'm going to drown myself. I can't stand it any longer.' Elizabeth tried to stop her but Hannah ran to the canal side near Fazeley Street and threw herself in and, by the time she

could be rescued, it was too late. When Hannah's mother heard of her death, she also tried to drown herself but James Wells only remarked, 'Oh, the ___, it would ha' been a good thing if she'd done it afore.' The coroner's inquest returned a verdict of suicide whist of unsound mind on the body of Hannah after condemning Royston for his depravity.

31 AUGUST 1884 Neighbours of Joseph and Emma Whittenham of Curzon Street were well aware that the marriage was not a happy one. Forty-six-year-old Emma was frequently seen with bruises inflicted by forty-two-year- iron moulder Joseph and witnesses later testified to hearing heated arguments between the couple. This Sunday a next-door neighbour named Julia Keefe heard Mr and Mrs Whittenham quarrelling and fighting for most of the day. At about half past nine this evening, the couple were upstairs when Mrs Keefe heard Joseph say, 'I'll break your _____ neck,' before a great noise on the stairs as though someone was falling. The next morning, Joseph called a doctor saying he could not rouse Emma but claiming he could remember nothing of the night before as he and Emma were very drunk. The doctor treated Emma but she died on 3 September without regaining consciousness. The post-mortem revealed that Emma had died due to extravasation of blood on the brain and Joseph was arrested on the charge of manslaughter. However, at the Birmingham Police Court, he was released without charge when it was decided there was not enough evidence against him. An angry mob attempted to attack Joseph's home when the verdict was announced but a police presence prevented any riotous proceedings.

SEPTEMBER

1 SEPTEMBER 1888 Knowing that she needed to go out, nineteen-year-old Ada Ferriday asked twelve-year-old Alfred Forrester and his sister, ten-year-old Alice, to look after six-month-old Minnie Ferriday (Ada's daughter) while she went to the market. The two children, who were Ada's cousins, came to the house at No. 2 Clifton Place, Asylum Road, Summer Lane, at about five o'clock this evening and Ada left shortly afterwards, leaving baby Minnie in her perambulator near the living room fire. The only other person in the house was Ada's father, Caleb Smith, who was 'the worse for beer' and sleeping it off in a nearby chair. When Ada returned about half an hour later, Alfred was gone but Alice was by the pram and immediately remarked that there was some blood on the floor. Ada picked up Minnie and noticed a deep cut around her right ankle so she took the child over to the doctor who stitched it. It was then discovered that Minnie's left ankle was so severely cut that the foot was only hanging on by a flap of skin. The baby girl was rushed to the General Hospital but died of blood loss soon after. A bloodied knife was found in the pram and Alice initially confessed to cutting the child after being told it would bring her good luck. Alfred and Alice were arrested on the charge of murdering Minnie but it soon became clear that Alfred had left soon after Ada went shopping and offered to pay Alice a penny to mind the baby. When Alice retracted her statement, suspicion fell on Caleb who was the only other person known to be in the room at the time of the attack. At the coroner's inquest, evidence suggested that Ada, Alfred, Alice or Caleb could have been responsible. However, experts disagreed whether children would have been able to inflict the injuries, Ada could not be placed at the scene and no one saw Caleb awake when there was the opportunity to harm Minnie. The jury had no alternative but to return a verdict of wilful murder against some person or persons unknown and baby Minnie was buried in a common grave at Warstone Lane.

2 SEPTEMBER 1902 Twenty-one-year-old stationer's manager Frank Saunders Gough believed he had found the woman of his dreams. Trying to attract Miss Turner's attention, Gough spoke to her and sent letters, explaining his love. Sadly, after initially showing some interest, the young lady's feeling cooled and she asked a friend to write a letter, telling Mr Gough that she did not desire to receive his communications. Gough, who was lodging at Strensham Road, Balsall Heath, was devastated by her refusal and, after obtaining a revolver, shot himself in the head on the evening of 1 September. Although he was still alive when discovered, Gough succumbed to lacerations to the brain this Tuesday morning. The inquest showed that he had written a letter to Miss Turner on the evening of the shooting, which read: 'If you like you can save me yet. If you don't come before ten o'clock it will be all over' which she didn't receive until too late. The jury returned a verdict of suicide whilst temporarily insane.

3 SEPTEMBER 1917 Minnie Lee returned to her house at No. 55 Henrietta Street this Monday afternoon with her seven-week-old daughter Hilda Winifred Lee after visiting relatives. Hearing voices upstairs, Minnie called up, thinking it was her husband James but was horrified when two men rushed down the stairs towards her. One of the men struck Minnie so that she fell to the floor still holding her daughter in her arms. As one of the men ran off, Minnie bravely grabbed at the other, who swung a metal jemmy at her before escaping into the street. Minnie laid Hilda down before chasing after the burglars, attracting the attention of her neighbours. When Minnie re-entered her home she was horrified to find Hilda dead. The child was taken to the General Hospital where it was revealed that Hilda's skull was fractured so badly that it had broken into two pieces. Thirty-six-year-old Thomas John Morris and thirty-seven-year-old Michael Galvin were arrested and charged with burglary and the murder of Hilda. At Birmingham Assizes on 7 December 1917, the two men admitted that they had broken into the Lee's house but denied seeing or striking the baby. Despite doctor Leather testifying that the injury to Hilda's skull might have been caused by a glancing blow of a jemmy or when Minnie fell to the floor, the jury found Morris and Galvin not guilty of murder or manslaughter. The two men were found guilty of burglary and each sentenced to three years' penal servitude.

4 SEPTEMBER 1880 When her neighbour, Sarah Freeth, was taken in by the police late on this Saturday night, thirty-six-year-old Mary Ann Partridge of Mount Street, Lodge Road, did not stand idly by. Instead she went to Mrs Freeth's house, collected the baby and walked with her to the police station. Upon her arrival at the station it seems that Mary Ann became rather abusive to PC Kelly and he arrested her for her behaviour. Mary Ann resisted the arrest, whereupon PC Kelly caught hold of her arm and threw her to the ground. When the two women were brought before magistrates on the Monday morning, Mary Ann complained of illness and a doctor was called but she worsened and died 10 September. At the inquest it was alleged that Kelly's violent assaulted had resulted in an inflammation of the abdomen and caused her death. A verdict of death from natural causes was returned but Kelly was severely censured for exceeding his duty.

5 SEPTEMBER 1861 Although six-year-old John Pickering was frequently told by his parents not to play near the canal, the young boy was last seen on the embankment of the Old Birmingham Canal this Thursday evening. When John did not return to his home in Spring Hill, his concerned parents alerted the authorities who dragged the water without success. However, three days later a man walking

along the canal side noticed the head of a child rise to the surface of the water. The body was much discoloured and swollen after spending so long in the water but it was identified as John. At the inquest, John's parents explained that their son enjoyed jumping from one boat to another and it was decided that he must have fallen in while attempting to do so.

6 **SEPTEMBER 1885** In December 1884, David Deeley Senior died and left the management of his estates to one of his younger sons called James. It seems that James decided that his brother – thirty-three-year-old David Junior – should take over the running of Windmill Farm near Quinton even though another brother – Charles – had taken an active part in its workings. Thirty-four-year-old Charles of Copsall Street, Birmingham took this in bad part and things came to a head when David's wife Mary began to make disparaging remarks about Charles' character. On this Sunday, Charles visited James at his farm in Ridgacre and, after spending a pleasant day, asked to stay the night after missing the Birmingham omnibus, something James was happy to agree to. Early on 7 September, Charles got up and, walking over to Windmill Farm, confronted Mary and David. 'I've come to take possession,' he said, to which Mary replied, 'I've got possession and we mean to keep it too.' At that Charles grabbed Mary's sewing machine and threw it into the yard, stating he would turn her and all of her possessions out. Mary grabbed at Charles and he beat her across the head before David came to his wife's defence. The two men began fighting violently until Charles broke free, pulled out a pistol and fired several times at Mary and David, hitting Mary in the hand, arm and scalp, and wounding David in the chest, arm and face. James, who had been alerted to the argument, found the couple seriously injured but alive. Charles, meanwhile, was lying on the ground with a bullet hole in the back of his throat where he had shot himself. The three were attended by surgeons but Charles died later that day from the bullet lodged in his brain. Mary made a full recovery but the injuries sustained by David caused his death in 1889.

7 **SEPTEMBER 1889** This Saturday afternoon saw the match between Packington Football Club and the Small Heath Reserves played at Fentham Road ground in Birchfield. In the second half, twenty-year-old Thomas Spittle, a promising player for Packington and well known in football circles, went in for a tackle against Richard Hall. The two players collided as they went for the ball, with Hall's knee catching Spittle in the abdomen and sending him to the floor. It quickly became apparent that Spittle was hurt and it was decided to send him to Birmingham General Hospital. Spittle, from Lennox Street, Lozells, initially seemed to rally but began to vomit violently and died

early Monday morning. The post-mortem revealed that Spittle's intestines had ruptured after being driven violently against his spine and were further damaged by the strain of vomiting. The inquest decided that Richard Hall's tackle was within the spirit of the game and returned a verdict of accidental death.

8 SEPTEMBER 1842 Samuel Davies, an employee of Mr Newbold, was working at Moseley Hall, making some repairs to the brick work on the outside of the house. To reach the damage the thirty-one-year-old painter was using scaffolding and, on this Thursday afternoon, he lost his balance and fell several feet to the ground. He landed on his stomach, on a large stone, and immediately started to complain of pain in his bowels. Davies was taken to his home in Skinner Lane where a medical man was called, finding him in a very exhausted condition and with agonising stomach pain. Despite all assistance, Davies died on Friday evening; the post-mortem revealed a ruptured colon, with one part almost torn through. The inquest returned a verdict of accidental death on the married father of three.

9 SEPTEMBER 1869 Twelve-year-old Harry Andrews of Irving Street was employed at the works of Mr Upton, printer of Great Charles Street, when he was sent on an errand to Crescent Wharf on this Thursday morning. No one is quite sure why but Harry decided to climb the crane there and, when he was some 30ft up, he suddenly slipped and plummeted to the ground. Harry sustained a fractured skull and several broken bones, dying of his injuries on the way to the Queen's Hospital.

10   SEPTEMBER 1878   This Tuesday afternoon an inquest was held on the death of ten-week-old James Hind. On 5 September, James' mother, Mary Hind, had come from Dudley to Birmingham but, unable to procure lodgings, had spent days walking the streets with the baby wrapped in her shawl. On Saturday evening, Mary realised that her illegitimate son was dead. The coroner, after revealing that the death resulted from suffocation – probably caused by the shawl pressed against Mary's breast – returned a verdict of accidental death.

11   SEPTEMBER 1886   After spending the afternoon selling toys with two of her siblings, nine-year-old Rebecca Surplice returned to her home in No. 5 Court, No. 4 House, Charles Henry Street, Deritend, at about half past eleven this Saturday night complaining of a 'sore tummy'. Rebecca began vomiting during the night and continued throughout the next day. Her mother noticed she was bringing up a great quantity of plum stones and took her to the Queen's Hospital where she received medicine. During the following week, Rebecca's condition worsened and she was admitted to the hospital on 20 September suffering from an obstruction in the intestines. An operation was performed where several fruit stones were removed but, although the operation seemed successful, Rebecca died twelve hours later. A post-mortem examination showed that the stones had perforated the intestines and disease had set in, causing peritonitis and death.

12   SEPTEMBER 1893   On 10 September, William Scattergood, a carter for Holmes' brewery, was making a delivery at the White Swan Inn at the corner of Cecil Street and Hanley Street when he was subjected to a seemingly unprovoked attack by two customers. Henry Davis and John Kinnersley launched a furious assault on Scattergood, knocking him to the ground and kicking him so hard in the face that his eye needed surgical treatment. Kate Glynn and Mary Coyne witnessed the fight but when they went to inform the landlord (who was standing watching nearby), Davis, Kinnersley and another man named Thomas Hugo rounded on them. Davis and Hugo took off their belts and used them to beat both women before all three men slapped, kicked and punched Kate and Mary before running from the scene. At Birmingham Police Court today, Davis was sentenced to four months' hard labour, Hugo three months in gaol and Kinnersley, because he had not used his belt on the women, also received three months – the magistrate further commenting on the unsatisfactory management of the public house.

13 SEPTEMBER 1878 Visitors leaving the Museum Concert Hall at about twenty minutes to eleven on the evening of 26 August 1878, noticed smoke coming from between the shutters of confectioner Joseph Dennison at St Martin's Digbeth. People rushed to alert the occupants and others were sent for the fire brigade when they realised that the fire had full possession of the ground floor and flames were seen licking at windows on the first floor. The noise seemed to have woken Dennison, for he appeared at a bedroom window with his wife, nineteen-year-old Julia Sarah, and their three-month-old son, Joseph Junior. A ladder was steered towards the window and Joseph Senior managed to scramble on to it, although flames were already making it difficult for the rescuers. Julia, who was holding her son, was too scared to get on the ladder so a man took the baby from her arms. However, in the chaos young Joseph slipped from his arms and fell to the street below, badly injured and seriously burnt. By now the heat was too strong and the men were driven back. Julia was overcome by the flames and she lost consciousness, tipped forward and falling from the window to her death. Two other women were spotted at another window and a blanket was brought round to try to get them to jump but neither did and eventually they vanished from sight. When the fire was brought under control, the bodies of fourteen-year-old Amelia Hand (Julia's sister) and sixteen-year-old servant Annie Brown were found in a back bedroom. When baby Joseph died in hospital the next morning there was a great deal of sympathy for Joseph Senior and condemnation for the slow reaction of the fire brigade but evidence came to light that suggested the fire was set deliberately. Suspicion fell on Joseph, particularly as he had just insured the property, and he was arrested. However, the inquest, held on this day, decided that there was not enough evidence to condemn Joseph and he was released.

14 SEPTEMBER 1890 Fifty-two-year-old Margaret O'Connor spent 13 September drinking beer alone at her home in No. 4 Court, No. 1 House, Henrietta Street. It is believed that as it became darker she lit a large paraffin lamp because some time later, when neighbours saw flames coming from a bedroom, they found the lamp broken at the top of the stairs. Margaret was in the room, her clothing on fire and horribly burnt on her face and body. Neighbours doused the flames but Mrs O'Connor was shockingly injured and died at the General Hospital on this day without explaining how the accident occurred.

15 SEPTEMBER 1887 This Thursday afternoon, Charles Alfred Clements from John Street, Smethwick was playing on the side of the canal in Lewisham Road. The nine-year-old illegitimate son of Lavinia Clements caught hold of the side of a boat and was clinging to it as it passed towards the lock. However, the boat suddenly swung closer to one side of the lock and Charles' chest and stomach were crushed on to the gate. Charles was taken to the Queen's Hospital but died the next day from terrible internal injuries. The inquest at the coroner's court returned a verdict of accidental death.

16 SEPTEMBER 1868 An inquest was held this Wednesday on the death of a newly born baby boy found in the canal near Tindall Bridge two days before. A rag was tied around the throat of the child, which suggested strangulation, but there was also a wound through the neck, which would have caused severe haemorrhaging. The surgeon who performed the post-mortem suggested that the boy would have lost a lot of blood through his untied umbilical cord and further gave the opinion that the neck wound was not accidental so the jury returned a verdict of wilful murder against some person unknown.

17 SEPTEMBER 1841 On the evening of 13 September, twenty-seven-year-old glass blower Joseph Avery and his sister Ann saw a swinging boat in Communication Row and decided to pay the half penny to take a ride. While they were in the boat, Joseph's shoe came off and, as he was trying to put it back on, he lost his grip as the ship swung upwards. Joseph was pitched over the heads of those in the boat and fell a distance of 4yds to the ground where he landed on the back of his head. Witnesses requested the boat be stopped but the men propelling it took no noticed and continued swinging until they felt the riders had had their full turn. Joseph was finally taken home to Bishopgate Street where a surgeon was sent for but he died of his head injuries early the next morning. The inquest, held on this day, returned a verdict of accidental death with a recommendation to the authorities to put a stop to such dangerous amusements.

18 SEPTEMBER 1883 Pearl button maker Jesse Ensor of Mill Street was passing Thomas Cuthbertson's house in Lancaster Street on 16 September when Thomas' cat ran out of the yard in front of Jesse, who threw a brick at it. The brick caught the cat on the head, causing such a serious injury that the cat had to be destroyed the next day. Thomas told Jesse he should be punished for what he had done to the cat as he loved it like one of his children, to which Jesse replied, 'If you do, I will serve you the same.' This afternoon the two men met and Jesse knocked Thomas down on a pile of stones, kicked him in the eye and threw bricks at his head until Thomas was knocked unconscious. Brought before Birmingham Police Court on 20 September, Jesse was sentenced to two months' imprisonment for the assault and one month for the cruelty to the cat.

19 SEPTEMBER 1868 American merchant Daniel Hasluck had done well for himself and was able to buy the Austins estate in Handsworth for himself and his family to live in. On this Saturday morning, Daniel's four children were in a boat on the pool, fishing with their nanny, when ten-year-old Blanche decided to swap seats. As she moved across, Blanche overbalanced and fell into the water, whereupon her fourteen-year-old brother Sidney Herbert jumped in to save her. The piercing screams of the other occupants of the boat alerted several servants, including twenty-three-year-old gardener Thomas Jenkinson who immediately entered the pool to help. Blanche was pulled back into the boat but Sidney, who was now struggling, grabbed hold of Thomas and the two sank under the water. By the time young Sidney and Thomas were found both were drowned.

20 SEPTEMBER 1859 At about half past six on the morning of 16 September 1859, Mary Jackson left her son Thomas Jackson asleep in his bed at their home in New John Street West. When she returned several hours later, eight-year-old Thomas was not in the house but Mary felt no particular alarm, believing him to be playing with friends. However, when he did not appear that night, Mary became worried and enlisted friends and neighbours in the hunt for her son but without success. On this Tuesday morning, labourer Edward Williams was loading sand from a sand bank in Wheeler Street when he unearthed a jacket, moments later a small hand also peaked from the bank. Horrified, Mr Williams fetched a policeman and between them they pulled out the body of Thomas Jackson. The post-mortem showed that Thomas had died from suffocation and it was believed that he was playing on the bank when he sank in. The inquest jury returned a verdict of accidental death.

21 SEPTEMBER 1895 After using bad language, twenty-two-year-old polisher Arthur Brown of Camden Drive was thrown out of his local public house by some of its customers on this evening. Seething at his ill treatment, Brown waited outside until fifty-two-year-old Edwin Wright left the drinking establishment and then pulled out a knife, stabbed Wright in the chest without provocation and ran from the scene. Police Sergeant Lambert administered first aid and took Edwin

to the Queen's Hospital while Brown was quickly apprehended. Brown was found guilty at Birmingham Quarter Sessions for wounding Wright; the assistant barrister said that there was not a single redeeming feature in the case and sentenced him to three years' imprisonment.

22 SEPTEMBER 1880 The much-respected Captain William Deakin was a member of an eminent firm of ironmasters and a magistrate in Birmingham. Sadly, in 1878 his fortunes somewhat reduced and the fifty-five-year-old began to avoid former acquaintances and moved to humble lodgings. For several years Captain Deakin had been courting twenty-eight-year-old Annie Inslay, who ran the Cup Inn, Bromsgrove Street, but recently she had expressed a desire to break their engagement, which Deakin took badly. On 22 September, he visited the Cup Inn several times in an attempt to change Annie's mind but she refused to do so. On the last visit, Deakin seemed to take the rejection well and asked Annie to pour him some beer, so she went to the cellar to draw some. When she returned to the bar, however, Deakin pointed a revolver at her and fired; the bullet missed and he fired again. This also missed but Annie fell to the floor in fear and Deakin, apparently under the belief he had killed Annie, put the gun to the side of the head and shot himself. The captain was taken to the Queen's Hospital but died there on 27 September.

23 SEPTEMBER 1886 Twenty-year-old kitchen maid Sarah Boyle had been working for Samuel Ellis, a schoolmaster at No. 7 St Augustine's Road, for two weeks when she went into the kitchen on 22 September to light the fire. After laying the firewood, Sarah lit it with a match but then decided to use some paraffin oil to ignite it properly. As she poured some oil on to the fire, the flames set the can alight, which exploded and doused the girl with burning liquid. Mr Ellis rushed downstairs and, finding Sarah burning from head to foot, he threw a blanket over the girl to dampen the flames and sent for a doctor. It was clear that Sarah was beyond help as her clothing was completely gone and her body was severely burnt; she was laid on the dining room sofa where she died within an hour. The inquest jury returned a verdict of accidental death on this day after the coroner expressed his concern on the improper usage of combustible liquids.

24 SEPTEMBER 1859 On this Saturday evening, forty-year-old toy maker Joseph Vernon met two strangers in Dale End who persuaded him to join them in a local public house in Chapel Street. The two men, who introduced themselves as axle-tree maker John Fox and hawker Thomas Perry, proceeded to get the extremely deaf Joseph

drunk and then, when they left the beerhouse, beat him around the face, stealing his remaining money. Joseph reported the attack and, at the Birmingham Police Court, Fox and Perry were charged with assault. Unfortunately, the only witness to the attack refused to attend so the two prisoners were discharged due to insufficient evidence.

25 SEPTEMBER 1861 At about eleven o'clock on the morning of 24 September, twelve-year-old John Bird from Park Street was grinding some tools at the Bordesley Mills, Adderley Street, where he was employed. Bird was using a steam-powered grinding stone which weighed over 3 tons when suddenly the stone broke into three pieces. Two of the pieces were propelled across the room, smashing into the walls and ceiling of the building, but the third struck John, breaking both his legs and fracturing his skull. Help was immediately called for but the boy died within minutes. The inquest jury on this day returned a verdict of accidental death on the unfortunate child.

26 SEPTEMBER 1891 When cabman Edward Albut was asked to drive a passenger to the Moseley New Pool at four o'clock this Saturday afternoon to watch a fishing contest, he decided to stop a while to watch the proceedings. After placing a rug and nose can on his horse, Albut left the cab and stood by the hedge where several boys were blackberrying. Suddenly something spooked the horse and it bolted towards Sare Hole Mill, galloping down the road and towards people enjoying a weekend stroll. Jumping into the hedge or ditch, everyone escaped serious injury except sixteen-year-old Elizabeth Eliza Alice Williams, who didn't see the vehicle approaching. The young teacher from Mayfield Terrace, Poplar Road, Sparkbrook, was struck on the back of the head by the right shaft of the cab, crushing her skull and pitching her to the floor where she died within moments. The inquest, determining that the horse had bolted due to some activity by the boys blackberrying, felt that Albut should not have left the cab unattended but decided Elizabeth's death was an accident and not manslaughter by any persons involved.

27 SEPTEMBER 1859 No. 22 Whittall Street was used by Messrs Pursall & Phillips as the premises for their percussion cap manufactory. The third floor housed the most dangerous part of the process, where ingredients were mixed together to make the detonating powder. At about eleven o'clock this Tuesday morning, some seventy workers were in the building when it was suddenly rocked by a deafening explosion. Neighbouring workers rushed to the scene to find a mass of timber, bricks and bodies. As attempts were made to rescue the survivors, brickwork continued to collapse, killing those underneath, and a fire began to rage, burning those unfortunately trapped in the wreckage. Parts of bodies were found, including an arm and a collarbone, but other parts were too burnt to be identified. Seventeen women and one man were killed in the explosion or died of their injuries; the youngest two being just eleven years old. The inquest could not conclusively prove the cause of the explosion but it was assumed that one of the highly combustible mixtures had ignited. Most of the dead were interred in nearby St Mary's church and a memorial was placed to commemorate the victims.

28 SEPTEMBER 1865 A well in a yard of Naden's Buildings adjoining the Acorn Tavern, Winson Green, had been out of repair for some time and several houses depended on its water supply. Early on this Thursday morning, pump maker fifty-nine-year-old Thomas Chirm and workmen Edward Lines and Charles Hadfield arrived to mend the pump, with twenty-two-year-old Lines descending the well. Normally a candle would be taken down to check for foul damp or carbonic gas but the well was relatively shallow and the men felt that there was little danger. Within a few minutes, however, it became apparent that something was the matter as Edward stopped working, there was a splash and he did not answer to any calls. Chirm then descended the well but, when he too did not respond to Hadfield's shouts, Hadfield ran for assistance. It was decided that no one else would climb down and instead grappling hooks were used. The bodies of Edward and Thomas were dragged up within twenty minutes, suffocated by carbonic gas. At the inquest, Chirm of Brearley Street West and Lines from Upper Tower Street were described as experienced pump men who were well aware of the dangers of foul damp and their deaths were accidental.

29 SEPTEMBER 1861 At half past one on this Sunday morning, forty-two-year-old wiredrawer John Thompson and Ann Walker, his forty-year-old mistress, knocked on the door of a bawdy house in Tanter Street owned by Emma Berresford. The couple, who were known to Emma, said they had been drinking at the Birmingham Onion Fair, felt it was too late to get to their home in Sutton Coldfield and asked for a bed. After sleeping at the house, John and Ann left to go drinking at the Engine Spirit Vaults in Stafford Street where a former lover engaged Ann in conversation, enraging John so much that he tried to assault Ann but was prevented. Ann then returned to Tanter Street and asked if she could lie down for a little while; Emma gave permission and, when John also appeared a short time later, she told him Ann was upstairs. John was overheard asking Ann to come home but she

refused and suddenly there was a loud scream. Emma, who rushed upstairs to find Ann bleed profusely from a neck wound and John holding a bloody knife, ran from the house shouting murder and John was quickly arrested. At the trial at Warwick Assizes on 17 December, it emerged that Ann had separated from her husband some three years before on account of her drunken habits and had lived with various men until meeting father-of-seven John some three months before. John was found guilty of the wilful murder of Ann while in a fit of jealousy. He showed penitence when executed by George 'Throttler' Smith in front of Warwick Gaol on 30 December, watched by a crowd of thousands.

30 SEPTEMBER 1865 Fourteen-year-old clerk Charles Robinson Jones of Bath Street was riding a horse along Summer Lane at about half past seven this Saturday evening when a boy suddenly ran up to him and struck the horse, causing it to spook and gallop down the street. Before Charles could regain control, the horse ran into a horse and cart and Charles was thrown under the wheels, crushing his pelvis and causing severe internal injuries. Conveyed to the General Hospital, Charles was given all available attention but died on 5 October. The inquest jury returned a verdict of manslaughter against the unknown boy who was never apprehended.

OCTOBER

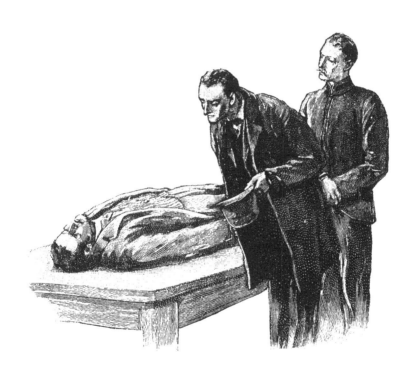

1 OCTOBER **1862** When sixteen-month-old William Butler from Aston Road developed a nasty cough, his mother, Emma, decided to visit druggist Mr Gillman of Gosta Green for a pennyworth of cough mixture. She was served by Mr Gillman's son, John, on this day, who told her to give a teaspoon of medicine to William each time he had a coughing fit. Emma took the bottle, which had no label, and over the day gave her son six doses of the medicine. She noticed William was extremely sleepy but felt no concern and the next day continued to dose the child. However, William fell into a deep sleep, stopped breathing and died on 2 October. The inquest returned a verdict of accidental death caused by overdosing on a drug, though the coroner felt Gillman showed gross neglect in not clearly explaining the danger of repeated doses.

2 OCTOBER **1873** At about midnight on this Friday evening, a night soil man was removing the contents of a foul open midden or cesspool near the Black Horse Inn on Oxford Street, when his pitchfork struck a solid object in the effluvia. The labourer pulled at the object, which proved to be the rotting corpse of thirty-five-year-old canal-side coal heaver Thomas Bishop who had been missing for over five weeks. Thomas, who was also known as 'Tommy Don't Care', was in an advanced state of decomposition, with his face almost eaten away, but his clothing and height made identification possible. Early indications suggested foul play, with a bloodied shirt, but further investigations told a different story. Tommy was last seen leaving the Black Horse in an extremely drunken state, heading down the court towards the cesspool. It is believed that he stumbled over the low wall of the midden, which had no other protection and suffocated in the waste.

3 OCTOBER **1893** Fifty-two-year-old Emma Hawkeswood of Hope Street had the misfortune to live in the same street as forty-seven-year-old gun maker John Harrison, a drunken and violent character. On the evening of 3 October, Emma, who was blind in the right eye, was standing talking to a neighbour when Harrison walked up to her and said, 'You ___ cow; go away from my house'. When Emma replied that she was not at his house, John pushed and kicked her before pulling her backwards by her hair. Emma fell to the floor, where John kicked her in the face, catching her left eye. After being rescued by the neighbours, Emma was taken to the General Hospital where it was discovered that her left eye was damaged beyond repair and had to be removed, meaning that she was now completely blind. Tried at Birmingham Quarter Sessions, John suggested that Emma had injured her eye by tripping on to a poker but was found guilty of inflicting grievous bodily harm and sentenced to three years' penal servitude.

4 OCTOBER **1869** At about three o'clock this Monday afternoon, a large workforce were on the scaffolding in front of the Oddfellows' Hall, Temple Street. The scaffolding was built on immense poles, placed in front of the building, but the construction proved insecure and it fell across the street, bringing down a portion of the wall about three storeys' high and carrying with it four of the workers. Seventeen-year-old John Wells was dug out unconscious, his skull fractured in several places, while eighteen-year-old labourer Charles Harris from Cheapside sustained broken arms, ribs and hip. Sarah Price, who was visiting some friends in Ludgate Hill, was caught in the debris, suffering a severe head wound which was compounded when the teeth of her comb were driven into her head. Over the next few days all three died of their injuries. The inquest determined that a section of cornice had fallen, carrying the brickwork with it, and returned a verdict of accidental death.

Temple Street. (Courtesy of W. Knowles)

5 OCTOBER **1878** Deciding that the easiest way across the canal was by means of an empty barge, fourteen-year-old Thomas Hannon of the Globe Yard, Dartmouth Street, climbed on to the boat near Pritchett Street. Unfortunately, while standing in the gangway of the cabin, he struck his head violently against a low wooden bridge erected over an arm of the canal, connected with Messrs Yates' works. Hannon was taken to the General Hospital after sustaining a fracture of the skull but died five hours later from his injuries. The inquest returned a verdict of accidental death.

6   OCTOBER 1887   After spending this Thursday evening in a local public house, thirty-year-old labourer Michael Lary returned to his house in Staniforth Street much the worse for drink and retired straight to bed. At about three o'clock the following morning, he woke feeling hungry so roused his wife Nora and demanded she prepare some supper. When she refused to make any food, Michael seized a large iron lock and threw it at her head, causing a severe scalp wound that needed hospital treatment. At Birmingham Police Court, Michael admitted a charge of assault and was sentenced to two months' hard labour.

7   OCTOBER 1843   Twenty-year-old Elizabeth King gave birth to her illegitimate daughter Mary in the workhouse in September 1843 but, as was their custom, the establishment turned her out today, a month after her confinement, despite having no means of support. King visited some neighbours in Ann Street who gave her food before she left. The next morning, she reappeared but without the baby and, when questioned, told witnesses that she had thrown Mary into the canal somewhere between the Cresent and Tyndall's bridges. King was taken into custody while the canal was dragged but the body of the baby girl was not found until a week later when it was spotted floating in a lock near Snowhill Bridge. At the coroner's inquest it

Inside the workhouse. (Author's collection)

was revealed that when King's mother had begged the workhouse to keep her longer, they had replied that they 'must turn out all the bitches together'. People who knew King described her as little better than an idiot, who had difficultly performing even basic tasks. When tried at Warwick Assizes it quickly became apparent that King was incapable of telling right from wrong and was acquitted of murder due to insanity and detained at Her Majesty's pleasure.

8 OCTOBER 1865 Although there was no previous ill feeling between twenty-five-year-old labourer John Clarke and twenty-year-old John Roach, both of Milk Street, a misunderstanding led to tragic consequences. Roach was drinking heavily this Sunday lunchtime when he became convinced Clarke was involved in attacking his brother the night before. Incensed, Roach went to Clarke's home and accused him of violence against his brother. Even though Roach denied all knowledge, Clarke thumped him twice in the stomach before leaving. Roach, who made no attempt to defend himself, seemed shaken by the attack and went to his sister's house where he became increasingly ill before suffering a fit, dying at about nine o'clock. Roach, hearing of Clarke's death, immediately gave himself up saying he remembered nothing. Tried at Warwick's winter assizes for manslaughter, John Roach was found not guilty when it emerged Clarke had been suffering from kidney disease and the medical evidence did not satisfactorily prove that Roach's blows were the cause of death.

9 OCTOBER 1882 By half past six this Monday morning, most of the men at Stephenson Tube Company, Liverpool Street, were busy at work when there was a terrific explosion in the boiler shed, followed by a shower of missiles and a cloud of seething steam. It quickly became clear that one of the boilers had exploded, killing fifty-three-year-old engine driver William Mewis on the spot. It seems that the married father of five had been shovelling coal into the fire hole when the force of the explosion drove him 12yds into a brick wall, crushing his head and body in the most shocking manner. Two other workers – twenty-year-old Henry Denston and nineteen-year-old Francis George Wilkins – were enveloped in the scalding steam; staggering out of the shed badly burnt before collapsing to the floor. Denston and Wilkins were removed to the General Hospital but died soon after. At the inquest it came to light that the boiler was reported unsafe prior to the explosion but chief engineer Henry Mosedale ordered only minor repairs. Mosedale was tried at Warwick Assizes in February 1883 for the manslaughter of the three men but the judge stopped the case, declaring that Mosedale's error of judgement was not sufficient to render him liable.

10 OCTOBER 1881 When the family of forty-four-year-old David Pullam decided that he needed the specialist care of the Borough Lunatic Asylum in Winson Green, his nephew had David admitted. On 10 October, Pullam was handed over to the care of forty-four-year-old attendant James Hughes. However, when the family visited him a mere three days later, they found David very ill and with several bruises on his body. David's wife, Elizabeth, told James that she feared her husband was dying but he laughed at her. Sadly, David declined rapidly and died that night. Two patients came forward to say that they had seen James pull David from his bed; bash his head against the wall before kicking him in the stomach. The post-mortem revealed that his death had resulted from peritonitis, shock and haemorrhage due to a ruptured bladder and James was committed for trial on the charge of manslaughter. At Warwick Assizes in February 1882, James explained that when he tried to get David out of bed so he could dress him, David refused and the two of them tussled but he did not attack David in the way suggested. Witnesses testified to James' good character and the jury decided to acquit him, feeling any injury on David was accidental.

11 OCTOBER 1895 At Birmingham Police Court on this day, William Bassett and his two sons, Leonard and John, were summoned for assaulting Richard Turley of Northumberland Street on 28 September 1895. On that Saturday night, Richard told the court that he had been walking home when the three men suddenly jumped him; John striking him a violent blow to the face while William hit him over the head with a weapon that caused a severe wound to the head. While Richard lay on the floor, he was repeatedly beaten and kicked until neighbours came to the rescue and took him home. However, William and his sons burst through the door and again attacked Richard, knocking over a lamp in the process so that the fire brigade was called. William Bassett explained to the court that Richard was in fact his son-in-law and had been attacked due to a brutal assault on his wife Sarah Turley née Bassett. The Bench dismissed Sarah Turley's complaint and fined John Bassett £1 or one month's imprisonment; William and Leonard were fined 10s or fourteen days.

12 OCTOBER 1878 This morning, eighteen-year-old Thomas Lock and his father left their home in Selly Oak and went to work on the threshing machine at Harborne Lane Farm. The pair set the engine and Thomas, climbing on to the top of the machine, went to remove a sliding board when his foot slipped into the revolving drum. Before the machine could be halted, Thomas' foot and leg were dragged through and severely crushed. Thomas was taken to the Queen's Hospital but he died of tetanus within days; the inquest jury returning a verdict of accidental death.

13 OCTOBER 1859 When twenty-year-old Caroline Goode left for a job in service on this day, she asked her landlady, Jane Parry, to take care of her infant daughter, Mary Ann. Mrs Parry readily agreed and was pleased to see how often Caroline visited her baby at her home in Milk Street, Digbeth. On 27 October, Caroline visited and asked to feed the little girl. However, Jane became concerned when she noticed that Mary Ann's food smelt strange and asked Caroline what she was doing, 'Good G__, Mrs Parry! I never put anything in it,' replied Goode and left. During the evening the baby turned purple and swollen but recovered when a doctor was called for. When Caroline visited again the little girl became ill once more but this time Mrs Parry kept some of the food and had it analysed, whereupon it was found to contain a large quantity of morphine. Goode was arrested and tried for attempted child murder at Warwick's winter assizes where she told a rambling story about Jane Parry's daughter accidentally poisoning Mary Ann and trying to blame her. The jury found her guilty and the judge passed sentence of death, which was later commuted to fifteen years' imprisonment.

14 OCTOBER 1891 A baby boy was born on this day to nineteen-year-old Emma Hanners of No. 8 Oxygen Street and her partner John Gardener. On 17 October, the unnamed infant was clearly hungry so John decided to soak some biscuits in water and fed his young son. Soon afterwards the baby began suffering convulsions and three days later the little boy was dead. At the inquest the doctor said that the child had died from improper feeding while John explained his belief that he thought the biscuits were proper food for the boy. After the jury returned a verdict of natural death the coroner summed up with a diatribe against the 'crass ignorance' of some people.

15 OCTOBER 1865 On the evening of 14 October, twenty-one-year-old bedstead fitter Francis Giles of Friston Street called into the King's Head in Pershore Street with several friends for some beer. Nineteen-year-old hawker Emanuel Henry Floris was already there, drinking and singing, when the two men got into a discussion about some money. When Giles left the public house, Emanuel followed him and, without another word, stabbed Giles in the left eye with a table fork. Giles was taken to the Queen's Hospital where, early this morning, the house surgeon attempted to remove the fork prongs that had broken off in the wound. Tried for unlawful wounding at Birmingham Borough Sessions in January 1866, Floris told the court that he was too drunk to remember anything. Nevertheless, he was found guilty and sentenced to twelve months' hard labour.

16 OCTOBER 1860 The crying of a baby would not normally attract the attention of a passer-by, but when it was heard on this Tuesday morning, coming from a dust-hole in a yard out of Bromsgrove Street, it could not be ignored. The baby boy was found completely naked except for a piece of coarse calico wrapped around his body and tied around the neck with string. Taken to the workhouse, the infant received every medical attention but weakened and died six days later. Mr Redfern Davies, surgeon at the workhouse, attributed the baby's death to congenital debility but was not prepared to say if it had been accelerated by the exposure to which the boy had been subjected. The inquest jury returned a verdict in line with the medical opinion.

17 OCTOBER 1865 Although fifty-two-year-old Margaret Burns and thirty-nine-year-old basket maker Martin Scahill had previously been credited with good character, by the time they began seeing each other in September 1865, both were known for their drunken habits. The couple moved into rooms in Chapel Street where they spent much of their time drinking and arguing. On 17 October, the argument turned violent when Martin accused Margaret of infidelity and threatened to leave. A fellow lodger then saw Martin knock Margaret to the floor where he put his foot on her chest, held her hair and beat her repeatedly around the head and body. The sounds of beating continued throughout the night and witnesses later reported hearing Margaret pleading, 'Oh, Martin don't ... don't hurt me ... I've £5 10s in the bed and if you will let me alone you shall have it.' The next morning a concerned neighbour offered to send for a doctor but Margaret asked for beer instead. She complained of dreadful pains in her stomach and head throughout the day and following night, finally dying at five o'clock on the morning of the 19th. Martin was arrested at a public house in Princess Street, and stood trial on 4 December 1865, where he readily admitted to attacking Margaret but denied intending to kill her. The post-mortem revealed Margret's body was covered in bruises, with internal injuries and a skull fracture that had resulted in lacerations to the brain. No evidence was given to show Martin had intended to kill Margaret, so the jury found him guilty of manslaughter and the judge sentenced him to five years' imprisonment.

18 OCTOBER 1888 Fifty-three-year-old labourer Samuel Bates of Allison Street was employed at the farm of A. Deakin at Hay Mills this Thursday. Samuel was trimming a wheat rick with a scythe blade when he somehow lost his balance and fell to the ground, catching his right thigh with the scythe as he fell. The blade inflicted a wound 3in in length and over 2in deep and he was taken to the Queen's Hospital

unconscious and bleeding heavily. Despite prompt treatment, the injury became infected and Samuel never regained consciousness – dying of exhaustion caused by the suppuration of the wound on 26 October.

19 OCTOBER 1887 When a fight between two women began in Park Street on 19 September, Emma Pollard decided to intervene. She separated the women but in the process Mrs Finn was rather roughly handled and, when thirty-two-year-old labourer Thomas Finn arrived, he took this rather badly. Before Emma could explain, Thomas said, 'I have got it in for you' and beat her unmercifully about the face and body. Emma's face was so disfigured she had to remain in the workhouse infirmary for a week and even at the trial at the Birmingham Police Court – held on this day – traces of the assault were still visible. Thomas Finn of Duddeston Row said that Emma was helplessly drunk on the night in question and caused the injuries when she fell. The court, after hearing that Thomas had been convicted ten times for violent assaults on females, found him guilty and sentenced him to two months' imprisonment with hard labour.

20 OCTOBER 1898 Mary Ann Aliban, a fifty-nine-year old spinster, lived alone at No. 60 Latimer Street and, although she lived frugally, it was commonly believed that she had a considerable amount of money stashed away at her house. This obviously proved tempting to thieves and Mary Ann awoke at seven o'clock on this Thursday morning to be confronted by two young men in her bedroom. She screamed in terror as they tied her to the bedposts before one of them took his handkerchief and gagged her. Unfortunately the handkerchief dislodged Miss Aliban's false teeth, forcing them down her throat and suffocating her. The criminals fled, taking a bag which was known to contain money.

Later in the day, Mary Ann was discovered and a neighbour recalled seeing two men leaving the property that morning. Suspicion fell on Claude Felix Mumby and James Twitty (alias George Webb) who fitted the descriptions. Mumby, a twenty-two-year-old brass finisher, was found with a large sum of money on his person and arrested soon after, but twenty-three-year-old Twitty evaded the police for several days until his arrest in Salford. Both men admitted they had been in Miss Aliban's house, having slept in the basement until early that morning. Mumby confessed to gagging Mary Ann but it had only been to prevent her screaming and he had had no intention of killing her. At Birmingham Assizes on 15 December, Mumby and Twitty were found guilty of the wilful murder of Mary Ann Aliban and sentenced to death; this, however, was later commuted to life imprisonment.

21 OCTOBER 1866 On the morning of 9 October 1866, Joseph Parker and his twenty-year-old son (also named Joseph) were working at their strip caster shop in Eyre Street, Spring Hill. In one corner was a pot of hot melting brass, suspended by a crane, which was being lowered when it suddenly slipped and poured the metal around Joseph Junior. His clothes ignited but he had the presence of mind to leap over the molten metal and throw himself into some water. Joseph was taken to the General Hospital at eleven o'clock where it was obvious he was badly burnt but no doctors attended him for over four hours when his burns were finally dressed. Young Joseph seemed to progress favourably until congestion of the lungs set in and he died on this Sunday afternoon. The inquest jury returned a verdict of accidental death but felt that some blame should be attached to the hospital for not attending to Joseph Parker sooner.

22 OCTOBER 1862 Catherine Keady and Amelia Homer were working together in one of the mixing buildings at Messrs Ludlow's percussion cap and cartridge manufactory in Aston Lane this Wednesday afternoon. The women were removing gunpowder from old cartridges and had approximately 2lbs of powder in front of them when it suddenly exploded. They were badly burnt around the face and torso, and were taken to the General Hospital where Amelia recovered but twenty-year-old Catherine succumbed to her injuries on 3 December. The coroner, after returning a verdict of accidental death, applauded the new system of lightly constructed buildings at such factories, as it meant that such an explosion did not result in the falling of heavy debris, which could cause further loss of life and damage to property.

23 OCTOBER 1847 After the death of her husband, Henry Wilkes, in April 1847, thirty-five-year-old Ann Wilkes was left in severely straightened circumstances. The widow and her four children – ten-year-old John Henry, seven-year-old Mary Jane Maria, six-year-old William Charles and four-year-old Frederick George – moved to Cheapside, Deritend, where Ann tried to set up a provision and tripe shop. The business failed and Ann took to selling belongings and pawning things to try to make ends meet. Unable to buy shoes and clothing for the family, it was clear that Ann was struggling financially and she decided to go to the workhouse to ask them to take the children so she could go into service. Afterwards, Ann complained to her mother that the people at the workhouse had pushed her around and wanted to take only two of the children. On this Saturday morning, Mr Edwards, a concerned neighbour, noticed that the shutters of the Wilkes' house were up and decided to enter the building. In the attic room he found the body of Frederick, his throat cut with a razor that was lying nearby. Ann lay nearby, bleeding heavily from a neck

Deritend. (Author's collection)

wound but still alive. The neighbour rushed into a bedroom and found the other three children dead; all with neck wounds. Ann was taken to the Queen's Hospital, where she admitted to killing the children as they slept because she could not afford to live anymore. She was to be committed for trial but died of her wounds on 28 October. Ann's inquest recorded that she had taken her own life and, despite the fact that those guilty of suicide were generally buried outside of consecrated ground, she was quietly laid to rest with her children at St Paul's churchyard.

24 OCTOBER 1871 This day saw the adjourned inquest on the deaths of two infant children found in a field in Handsworth. On 14 October, John Powell was walking along Hill Road when his attention was attracted by a piece of old bed linen lying close to the road. When he went to pick it up, John was horrified to find the bodies of a baby boy and girl inside. The post-mortem revealed that the male infant was stillborn but the baby girl had lived for a few minutes, dying from a lack of proper attention. The coroner expressed his regret that cases of this description occurred so frequently around Handsworth, but felt that they were unlikely to find the persons implicated.

25 OCTOBER 1868 When Emma Boden married labourer Robert Washington, the marriage initially seemed a happy one. However, by October 1868, Emma had returned to the protection of her guardian, John Field, a brass caster living in Park Road, due to Robert's ill treatment. On 24 October, thirty-four-year-old Robert visited his wife but she told him that she wanted nothing more to do with him, suggesting that she took care of one of their children while he took in the other.

Robert stormed from the house declaring: 'You or me or someone else will fall to the ground before the night is out.' Later that evening, Robert and John Field were both drinking in the Abbey Tavern and when John left, Robert followed him. At about one o'clock this morning, as John was lying on his sofa, Robert rushed in with a pocketknife and stabbed him twice in the face. The commotion was heard in the street and John was able to prevent further injury until Robert was arrested. Tried at Birmingham Police Sessions for wilful stabbing, Robert claimed that he had received ill treatment at the hands of John while in the Abbey Tavern but he was committed to the quarter sessions and sentenced to six months' imprisonment.

26   OCTOBER 1858   Twelve-year-old Jane Macguire lived with her parents in a court in Lawrence Street and, at ten o'clock this evening, she went to their neighbour, John Phillips, a shoemaker, to get a pair of her father's boots mended. John, who was described as a dirty-looking old fellow, completed the job and asked Jane to bring back some shavings to light his fire, which she agreed to do. However, when she returned to his house, John pulled her to the ground and tried to forcibly remove her clothing. Luckily for Jane, her mother came to see why she was taking so long and prevented any further assault. Brought before the police court the next day, John admitted acting with some indecency but said that he had had no criminal intention and it was Jane who was first free with him by pulling at his hair. The court, however, found the thirty-eight-year-old shoemaker guilty of indecent assault with intent and fined him 40s or six weeks' hard labour if he failed to pay.

27   OCTOBER 1897   At about three o'clock this Wednesday afternoon, thirty-five-year-old Frederick Frank Chappell of Park Road, Saltley, was at work at A.R. Dean, house furnishers and decorator of Corporation Street. As a porter, part of his role was to move furniture between the different floors using the lift, and on this day, five bags of horsehair were to be taken from the ground floor to the third floor. Chappell decided to put all five bags in the lift cage and do the trip in one. This did mean that there wasn't enough space for him to travel up in the lift as well but he used the stairs and met the cage when it reached the third floor. Opening the cage door, Chappell leant in to unload the horsehair but fell forward, lying half in the lift and half out. Unable to control the lift, it continued to move upwards and Chappell – failing to escape in time – was trapped between the floor of the lift and the top of the doorframe, crushing his skull and neck. Colleagues rushed to release him but he suffocated before they were able to help. At the inquest, A.R. Dean explained that it was against company policy to use the lift in this way and a verdict of accidental death was given.

28 OCTOBER 1884 Sixteen-month-old Annie Elizabeth Lloyd had always been a delicate child but her health took a turn for the worse in October 1884. Her mother, Ann Lloyd, told neighbours that, according to the doctor, nothing more could be done and baby Annie was dying. On this Tuesday morning, a friend visited the Lloyds at their home at No. 7 Stour Street, Ladywood, and found Annie lying by the fire. The friend advised Ann to prepare an upstairs room and move Annie away from the fire so, according to Ann, she put a gown in front of the fire and went upstairs, leaving her daughter where she was. Suddenly noticing smoke, Ann rushed down and saw that the gown was on fire, part of which had fallen on the baby's blanket, setting it alight and burning Annie on the right side of her body and face. A doctor was called but Annie died of her injuries that evening. At the inquest it was revealed that Ann had insured the child and received money on Annie's death, but the jury decided the fire was accidental.

29 OCTOBER 1895 Horrified to find herself pregnant for the sixth time, thirty-three-year-old Rebecca Simister decided on drastic action. After approaching her doctor for an abortion, which he refused to undertake, Rebecca turned to fifty-seven-year-old midwife Sarah Eden for help. On 23 October, Rebecca left her house in High Street Aston without telling her husband Thomas where she was going. She returned later, complaining of feeling unwell and the next morning she told Thomas she had miscarried but didn't need to see a doctor. By the 25th, Rebecca was too ill to leave her bed but asked her husband to fetch the midwife. When Sarah arrived it became clear that she had assisted Rebecca in causing a miscarriage but begged Thomas not to tell anyone as no instruments had been used. A doctor was sent for, who became suspicious, and Rebecca confessed to an abortion before dying on 29 October. The post-mortem revealed that Mrs Simister had died from blood poisoning caused by a punctured womb and intestines. Sarah Eden was arrested and tried on 10 December at Warwickshire Assizes for wilful murder. The jury found her guilty and the judge, Mr Justice Day, sentenced her to death after commenting that she had been justly convicted. This sentence was later commuted to penal servitude for life.

30 OCTOBER 1888 At Birmingham Quarter Sessions on this day, slogging gang members' nineteen-year-old stoker George Betts and eighteen-year-old filer James Simpson were charged with maliciously inflicting grievous bodily harm on PC James Brown and Laura Sanders. On the evening of 2 October, Betts and Simpson were in Aston Road with several other members of the gang when Betts spotted PC Sanders across the road. He went over to her and, after making insulting remarks, knocked

her down. PC Brown arrived at the scene and tried to take Sanders to hospital but was followed by the gang who pelted him with stones. One stone struck Brown on the head and he fell to the floor, whereupon Simpson hit him with a brick. Other police officers arrived and conveyed Sanders and Brown to the General Hospital where they remained for several days. The jury found Betts and Simpson guilty of the charge and the two men were each sentenced to fifteen months' imprisonment with hard labour.

31 OCTOBER 1888 Sometime in June 1888, forty-year-old American Charles McLean called at the house of Eliza Paris in Broad Street. McLean explained to Mrs Paris that he was a doctor of divine science and encouraged her to attend some of his seminars, which she duly did with her thirteen-year-old daughter Gertrude Eliza Paris. At each of the meetings, McLean commented on how ill Gertrude looked and begged permission to examine her to ascertain the problem as he was a medical man. In July, McLean made a preliminary examination on Gertrude and told Mrs Paris that he had discovered an internal obstruction which, unless removed, would kill her daughter within three months. Much alarmed, Mrs Paris agreed for McLean to see Gertrude and, on 29 July, he returned to the house. Charles Mclean stripped Gertrude naked and, after asking Mrs Paris to leave the room, indecently assaulted the young girl. On 8 August another 'examination' took place but when Gertrude told her mother what was happening, Mrs Paris called the police. Tried at Birmingham Quarter Sessions on 31 October 1888 for indecent assault and ill treatment, McLean denied all charges and accused Mrs Paris and her daughter of extortion and blackmail. The jury, however, found him guilty and, after being described as 'a hypocrite of the most disgusting and repulsive type', sentenced him to five years' penal servitude.

NOVEMBER

1 NOVEMBER 1838 The inquest on the death of eighteen-year-old Mary Ann Evans of Milk Street, Aston, was held today. Mary Ann was being courted by twenty-year-old file cutter Abraham Hollyoakes and, on the evening of 30 October, the pair spent the evening together at her mother's house. At about one o'clock the next morning, the couple left but, just an hour later, witnesses testified to finding Abraham standing by the canal at Great Barr Street Bridge, soaking wet and alone. When questioned, he said that he had fallen in the water, mentioning that Mary Ann had also fallen in but climbed out and gone home. Returning to Milk Street, there was no sign of the girl and it was then that Abraham told neighbours that he and Mary Ann had made a suicide pact and she was dead in the canal. Sure enough the body of Miss Evans was found in the canal but, due to Abraham's inconsistent story, he was arrested. At the inquest, Abraham told the court that Mary Ann and her mother had argued and, being unhappy, the pair had decided to drown together to escape their sorrows. The jury felt that this was a feeble cover for murder and the case was assigned to the Warwick Assizes. However, in March 1839, Abraham Hollyoakes was found not guilty of the wilful murder of Mary Ann when the jury decided that there was no evidence to prove Abraham had forced the girl into the water.

2 NOVEMBER 1892 This day saw the coroner's inquest on the death of forty-year-old shoemaker William Workman. On 29 October, a police officer living in Ventnor Road, Hockley, was informed by a neighbour that a serious affray was taking place further down the street. PC Shaw made his way to the house where he found nineteen-year-old William Workman, who pointed to the body of his father in the hall. Shaw found William Senior bleeding heavily from a neck wound but it quickly became apparent that he was dead. William Junior admitted attacking his father after he heard him threatening to kill his mother. He told the police that he had confronted William Senior and, when his father picked up a knife and rushed at him, he grabbed at the uplifted hand and the blade entered his father's throat. At the inquest, evidence was produced which testified to William Senior's violent and aggressive nature. Witnesses described how the family had tried to turn him from his criminal activities and it is believed that his wife found him producing false coins on the fatal night and threatened to tell the police. The jury returned a verdict of homicide through misadventure and William Junior was released.

3 NOVEMBER 1872 A disagreement between twenty-year-old musician Charles Gilcher and Gustave Kuglin descended into violence this Sunday evening. Gilcher, accompanied by two friends, went to Kuglin's house in Bordesley Street and

demanded that Kuglin fight them. Kuglin refused and was closing the door when Gilcher rushed through, stabbing Kuglin's wife Jane in the hand with a knife. Kuglin was stabbed in the face and a friend named Fanny Drew was also injured before Gilcher left. The police were called who arrested Gilcher for the attacks. At Birmingham Police Court, Gilcher was found guilty of stabbing and committed for four months.

4 NOVEMBER 1850 On 29 October 1850, forty-two-year-old surgeon Jonathan Gilby Devis of Temple-Place, Bath Row, was engaged in making a post-mortem examination of the remains of a female who had died soon after childbirth. At the conclusion of the examination, Devis accidentally pricked one of his fingers with the needle which had been used in sewing up the incisions, and shortly afterwards his hand became violently inflamed. Jonathan received treatment from fellow medical professionals but mortification set in and he died on this day. The inquest jury returned a verdict of accidental death on the unfortunate Devis.

5 NOVEMBER 1850 At about one o'clock this Tuesday afternoon, a boatman travelling along the Old Birmingham Canal near Snowhill tunnel suddenly observed a hand appear on the surface of the water before disappearing. Using a rake, the body of fourteen-year-old Thomas Smith of Fleet Street was dragged from the canal; the lad was last seen over a week before when he left with a man called Van to work at the collieries. According to the statement of the mysterious Van, he had parted from Thomas in Baggot Street on the evening of 29 October. However, when Van subsequently told a different story and the post-mortem revealed a substantial head injury on the body of young Thomas, the inquest was adjoined until 8 November. In the event, the surgeon could not say if the injuries were received before or after immersion in the canal and it was decided that Thomas had wandered into the canal while tired.

6 NOVEMBER 1884 Although forty-eight-year-old Thomas Rice was a wheelwright by trade, he kept a paraffin shop near his home in Aston Road North where he lived with his forty-six-year-old wife Mary Ann. The couple, according to a servant, were constantly quarrelling and Thomas would assault his wife and children violently when crossed. Early on this Thursday morning, Thomas was about to knock one of his daughters downstairs when Mary Ann interfered and Thomas hit her before smashing up some furniture. At dinnertime, Thomas was in the kitchen emptying a bucket of paraffin when Mary Ann entered. Without provocation, Thomas said, 'I will settle you,' and threw the paraffin over his wife who was standing near the fire. Mary Ann's dress immediately set alight and she ran screaming into the yard

where neighbours doused the flames. Thomas was arrested while Mary Ann was taken to the General Hospital but, burnt over much of her body, she died in agony on 18 November. Tried for manslaughter at Birmingham Assizes in February 1885, Thomas was found guilty and sentenced to just nine months' imprisonment.

7 **NOVEMBER** 1893 At Birmingham Police Court on this day, fifteen-year-old sailor boy Oliver Phillips of Woodcock Street was charged with stabbing horse keeper Arthur Turrell in a stable in Adderley Road, Saltley. On 23 October, Turrell was working in the loft at the Anglo-American Oil Company's stable when Phillips came in for a horse but began throwing manure at the white-washed walls. Justifiably annoyed, Turrell descended the loft steps and tried to stop him; the two exchanged blows before Phillips pulled out a pocketknife, challenged Turrell to a fight and stabbed him in the left side. Turrell collapsed with blood loss and he had to be taken to the General Hospital while Phillips was arrested. Phillips freely admitted to the assault but claimed it was done in a struggle and quite accidentally; the magistrates referred the case to Birmingham Quarter Sessions where he was bound over to his uncle's charge and released.

8 **NOVEMBER** 1902 Twenty-three-year-old Albert Capewell had never recovered from the guilt of causing his mother's death and drowned himself in the canal near Witton Cemetery on this day. At his inquest it was revealed that in 1891, Albert's

Witton Cemetery. (Author's collection)

brother Frederick Capewell had brought a breech-loading pistol from a co-worker. On the afternoon of 23 November 1891, Frederick's wife Emma took the gun round to the house of Frederick and Albert's parents in Hatchett Street but found only their forty-seven-year-old mother Jane at home. The two women looked at the pistol for a while then wrapped it in paper and placed it on a shelf. Not long afterwards, Albert returned home from school and, hearing about the pistol, took it off the shelf to look at it more closely. Despite his mother asking him not to play with the gun, Albert cocked the trigger and was pointing it when the pistol slipped from his hands and went off, shooting Jane through the neck. She immediately fell to the floor – blood rushing from her mouth and nose – and by the time she was taken to the General Hospital she was insensible, dying soon after. Albert was arrested for the manslaughter of Jane Capewell but it was agreed that the shooting was an accident and he was released. The coroner returned a verdict of suicide while of unsound mind on poor Albert.

9   NOVEMBER 1870 After many years alone, twenty-nine-year-old screw maker Mary Filleburne believed she had finally found love with labourer John Davies. On 5 November, Mary, in the company of her landlady Mrs Potterton, left her lodgings in Allison Street to visit the King's Head public house in the same road and, while they were there, John came in. Mary invited John to join the group but he just walked up to them, tasted the beer and then passed to another room without exchanging a single

Birmingham and Fazeley Canel–Fazeley Junction today. (Author's collection)

word with Mary. Distraught, Mary told Mrs Potterton that she would destroy herself if her young man did not speak to her. Shortly afterwards Mary went missing but was seen by a neighbour walking down Fazeley Street. Early the next morning, Mary's body was found floating in the canal near Fazeley Street Bridge. The inquest today, finding no evidence of foul play, returned a verdict of suicide whilst in a state of insanity.

10 NOVEMBER 1841 When neighbour Jane Eaves entered fifty-year-old Hannah Weale's home in Summer Street on 9 November, she was concerned to see how oddly Hannah was behaving. Hannah was washing clothes but seemed to be doing it all out of order. Jane remarked on this, to which Hannah replied, 'I am a foolish woman, I wish someone would dash my brains out.' Jane, who later told the court that Hannah had been in low spirits for several months, left without real concern. At about four o'clock this Thursday afternoon, however, Hannah's daughter came to Jane's house, saying that her home was all locked up. Jane went across with another neighbour and spotted Hannah at an upstairs window, undressed with her hair thrown over her face. Jane's husband broke down the front door and they rushed upstairs. Hannah was sitting on a chair; a throat wound over 2in long on her neck and blood all over the floor. Help was sent for but Hannah died within half an hour. The inquest jury returned a verdict of suicide while temporarily insane.

11 NOVEMBER 1884 On this Tuesday morning, two-year-old Rose Taylor was sitting at breakfast at her home in Woodbine Terrace, Alcester Street, when she spilled a cup of scalding tea over herself. Her mother Emily Taylor applied a homemade remedy of linseed oil and lime-water poultices to the burns but, when she went to work, Rose was left alone, playing out in the yard. On Friday, Rose took a turn for the worse and died that evening. At the inquest, the coroner asked Mrs Taylor why she did not seek medical attention and she replied that she thought she could look after Rose herself. Medical evidence suggested that Rose had died from congestion of the lungs caused by scalding and exposure to the cold air so a verdict of accidental death was returned; the coroner remarking that he did not wish to censure the mother whose stupidity even the gods contended in vain.

12 NOVEMBER 1877 When William Smith was brought before Birmingham Police Court charged with being drunk and disorderly, it seemed an open-and-shut case but Smith told a different story which was collaborated by witnesses. On this Monday evening, Smith was standing in Summer Lane with a friend when PC James Bailey walked up to him and said, 'You ___, I've a charge against you,' and took him into custody. As they were walking down Great Hampton Row, Constable Bailey threw Smith on the paving stones, got hold of him by the ears and violently dashed his head against the pavement until he was almost knocked senseless. At an adjoined trial Bailey denied this, saying Smith had resisted arrest and thumped him in the face, but when the court heard that PC Bailey had already been reported fifteen times in the last eight months, they decided he was not fit to be a police officer and he was discharged from the force. With regards to Smith, the Bench remarked that he was of a very bad character and had been before the court fourteen times before, but for the present offence he had been sufficiently punished and was discharged.

13 NOVEMBER 1843 In August 1843, gun finisher Abraham Hassall left his heavily pregnant wife and began cohabitating with another woman. Left to fend for herself, twenty-three-year-old Hannah Hassall and her five children moved into lodgings in William Street North. Hannah met Abraham on several occasions throughout October and each time he treated her extremely roughly, even kicking her in the stomach just weeks before she was due to give birth. Hannah was unable to sit properly after the final assault and, when she gave birth on 25 October, the baby boy was dead. According to the doctor, the state of decomposition showed that the baby had died at least three weeks before. After initially recovering from the birth, Hannah began showing signs of internal infection, with stomach pains, diarrhoea and a high temperature, eventually dying early this morning. At the inquest, the post-mortem revealed that Hannah had an abscess on her uterus which the surgeon believed had caused her death so, with a lack of witnesses to show that it was Abraham who kicked his wife, the jury returned a verdict of death by the visitation of God. After the coroner issued a caution to Abraham on his behaviour, Abraham told the court that Hannah's brother was threatening him. The coroner said that the law would protect him.

14 NOVEMBER 1885 Although forty-one-year-old varnish mixer Henry John Lea of Ladywood Road had twice been imprisoned for indecent behaviour towards young girls, it did not stop his actions on this day or the following three days. Lea hung around Wheeley's Lane and, whenever a girl appeared alone and without adult company, he exposed himself and tried to encourage her to follow him. Unsurprisingly,

after four girls reported a similar incident to their parents, Lea was tracked down. Tried at the police court in December 1885, the stipendiary said that children needed to be protected from such things and sentenced Lea to two separate terms of three months in gaol.

15 NOVEMBER 1865 Forty-five-year-old William Cook of Scholefield Street, Aston worked at the Britannia Works, Aston, as a smith. At about half past five this Wednesday afternoon, Cook was engaged in forging a piece of iron under a steam hammer. For some reason the hammer struck the side of the iron, causing it to bounce up and hit Cook's head. The weight of the metal threw him to the floor, fracturing his skull in several places and crushing his nose and eye socket. Cook was rushed to the General Hospital but his injuries were so serious he never regained consciousness and died on 17 November. The inquest jury returned a verdict of accidental death.

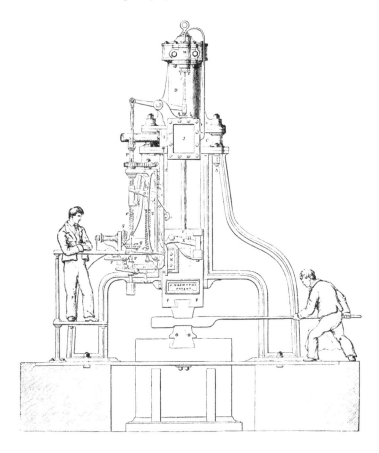

The Nasmyth Steam Hammer. (Author's collection)

16 NOVEMBER 1885 At about eleven o'clock this Monday morning, forty-four-year-old fulminate manufacturer George Hinks was working in the wet-fulminate shed at his home in Cotterills Lane, Alum Rock, when there was a sudden explosion. George's wife Sarah rushed to scene, where she found her husband badly injured amongst the debris of the shed. Hinks was rushed to hospital but his toes and right hand were blown off, his thighs badly lacerated and his abdomen terribly scorched; he died of his injuries later that day. The inquest returned a verdict of accidental death.

17 NOVEMBER 1890 On the evening of 8 November 1890, forty-eight-year-old glass cutter Samuel Case returned to his home in Burton Place, Cowper Street, after drinking for several hours. His wife Elizabeth saw that Samuel was in 'a strange mood' and decided to go to bed, but as she passed him, he hit her around the back of the head with his fist. Forty-year-old Elizabeth took her seven children and they barricaded themselves in another room, leaning against the door to prevent Samuel's entrance. However, Samuel continued to batter at the panels of the door until one gave way and he was able to grab Elizabeth's head. Pulling her neck back, Samuel drew a knife across Elizabeth's throat three times as the children watched, screaming in terror. Without a word, Samuel left the room and some of the children placed clothing around their

mother's neck to staunch the bleeding. Neighbours, alerted by the screams, called for the police and a doctor, and Samuel was arrested. Luckily for Elizabeth, the knife was blunt and the wounds were superficial. Brought before the Birmingham Police Court on this day, Samuel was charged with attempted murder and committed to the December assizes, where he pleaded guilty to wounding, blaming the attack on beer and provocation. The judge said he had not an atom of sympathy for Samuel but, taking into consideration Samuel's wife and children and the hardship they would endure without Samuel's wage, sentenced him to eighteen months' hard labour.

18 NOVEMBER 1890 Kate Clifford had recently separated from her husband and was living at No. 7 Court, No. 1 House, Phillips Street, Aston, with her children, including seven-month-old daughter Emma. On this Tuesday morning, Kate put Emma to bed and then went to a pledge shop in the Aston Road before embarking on a drunken afternoon with friends. When Kate returned at four o'clock, she noticed that something was wrong with Emma and sent for a doctor who declared the baby was dead. At the inquest it became clear that Kate was a drunkard who frequently neglected her children and it was reported that, when her son asked for money to buy bread, she told him she would kick out his intestines if he bothered her further. The post-mortem doctor found Emma to be dirty and horribly wasted, dying from convulsions. The jury returned a verdict of death from natural causes and desired the coroner to censure Mrs Clifford.

19 NOVEMBER 1892 When thirteen-year-old matchgirl Annie Edkins became a servant in the Rann household in Stafford Street on this day, she must have been pleased with her change of circumstances. However, on the evening of 23 December 1892, eleven-year-old Malcolm Rann overheard his father and mother – forty-eight-year-old army pensioner Thomas and thirty-year-old Elizabeth – talking about how they were going to abuse the young girl. Later that day, Annie was sent to get whiskey, which she and Elizabeth drank together. Mrs Rann then dragged Annie to her room, threw her on the bed and held her there while Thomas raped her. Annie reported the assault but Thomas claimed it was a blackmail attempt. However, it was clear that Annie had been attacked and the Rann couple were arrested; Thomas charged with rape and Elizabeth with aiding and abetting. At Birmingham Assizes in March 1893, Justice Bowen remarked that it was one of the worst cases he had ever heard and sentenced Mr Rann to twenty years and his wife to fifteen years' penal servitude.

20 NOVEMBER 1885 The mood at the Crown and Anchor Inn, Gem Street, was friendly on 19 October when a group of patrons began dancing in the bar. In the process, a man named Saunders accidentally knocked a glass over and broke it so twenty-seven-year-old striker Matthew Marney decided to solicit subscriptions to compensate the landlord. Holding the broken tumbler, Marney went round with his hat, asking men for a halfpenny, but when he reached thirty-four-year-old Thomas McGuire, McGuire told him he hadn't got one. Marney rubbed the glass on McGuire's face whereupon McGuire told Marney to take the tumbler away or he would smash it over the striker's head. At that Marney struck the glass against McGuire's neck, leaving a wound 3in in length and severing the jugular vein. McGuire was taken to the General Hospital but he bled to death within minutes. Marney gave himself up to police and was tried for manslaughter at Warwickshire Assizes on 20 November, where he was found guilty and sentenced to ten months' hard labour.

21 NOVEMBER 1893 Mary Ann Neal was preparing vegetables at her home in Wellington Road, Perry Barr, on 12 November, and laid a pan of boiling water on the floor while she was doing so. Her son, four-year-old Charles, was looking after his five-week-old brother Horace and, as he passed the pan, he accidentally dropped Horace into it. The baby was taken to the General Hospital where he was found to be severely scalded on the upper body and, despite initially making good progress, Horace died on this Tuesday. A verdict of accidental death was returned.

22 NOVEMBER 1843 The inquest on the death of servant Ann Grant was held on this day at the Old Crown, Deritend. On 20 November, Ann, who lived in Tamworth, had arranged to meet friends at the Bull Ring but, as she wasn't familiar with Birmingham, was unsure of her directions. As she was walking down Lady Pool Lane, she met John Marygold who told her he was going to the Bull Ring and would take her in the right direction. However, when they reached the Coach and Horses, Ann suddenly exclaimed, 'Good God! Look at my foot, how the blood comes. I doubt my leg has burst!' John saw blood pouring furiously from her foot and said she ought to rest at the inn but she refused, saying her friends were waiting. They had just reached the Old Crown when Ann collapsed, dying just five minutes later. Surgeon, Mr Archer told the inquest that Ann had died from loss of blood occasioned from the bursting of a blood vessel where she had an ulcer. The jury returned a verdict of death by the visitation of God.

23 NOVEMBER 1860 Twenty-year-old Elizabeth Allen of Moseley Street was working on one of the lathes at Alderman Cox's works on this Friday afternoon when, as she leant over the machinery, part of her dress became entangled in the shafts. Before Elizabeth could free herself, she was dragged in and whirled around the shaft several times. By the time she was rescued, Elizabeth, who had sustained serious internal injuries and many broken bones, was dead. An inquest held on 26 November returned a verdict of accidental death for Miss Allen but attributed the death to the large crinoline she was wearing at the time.

24 NOVEMBER 1866 The inquest on the death of thirty-nine-year-old Eliza Kerenhappuch Hampton of Nursery Terrace, Hunter's Lane, was held today. On the morning of 23 November, her son Samuel was woken by a loud report coming from the bedroom of his parents. Rushing in, Samuel found Eliza dead on the bed and his father, thirty-eight-year-old engraver John Wallis Hampton, with a hole in his chest just above his heart. John was alive and told Samuel that he had strangled Eliza in a fit of jealously then shot himself with the 'mini cannon'. A doctor was called, who ascertained that Eliza had been dead for some hours, and John was rushed to the General Hospital where he lingered for five days before dying of his injuries. Witnesses testified to John Hampton's obsession with Eliza's supposed infidelities. He seemed to have been finally tipped into insanity when his wife revealed that she was pregnant with their eighth child and John told friends and relatives that the child was not his. The jury returned a verdict that Eliza was wilfully murdered by John who then committed suicide while of unsound mind.

25 NOVEMBER 1871 Fifty-one-year-old wagon maker Frederick Oakes was a heavy drinker who often argued with his wife Catherine when drunk. On this Saturday morning, neighbours heard shouting coming from the Oakes' house in No. 1 Brighton Place, Garrison Lane, where Frederick was demanding money for beer from fifty-four-year-old Catherine but she was refusing to give him any. At about eight o'clock, neighbour Mary Brooks saw Mr Oakes hitting his wife and attempted to intervene but, ten minutes after she left, there was a scream and Catherine staggered out of her home bleeding profusely from a deep wound across her throat. Before a doctor could be fetched, Catherine, whose windpipe was completely severed, bled to death. Police entered the house and found Frederick sitting on a chair in a pool of blood, a large carving knife in his hand and his throat cut from ear to ear. Still alive, Mr Oakes was taken to the Queen's Hospital but he never spoke about why he had killed his wife, dying two days later. The coroner's inquest returned a verdict of wilful murder on the body of Catherine and recorded that Frederick had committed suicide whilst in a state of insanity.

26 NOVEMBER 1860 After supervising the erection of an apparatus for grinding cinders at the Fazeley Street Mills in Digbeth, fifty-five-year-old Bryan Feeney remained in charge of the machine. At about five o'clock this Monday evening, Feeney was seen at work near the revolving stone but, by nine o'clock, fellow workers realised that he was missing. Searchers were horrified to discover his mutilated remains lying in the groove where the crushing stones revolved round. The inquest jury returned a verdict of accidental death, taking comfort in the fact that Feeney's death would probably have been instantaneous.

27 NOVEMBER 1881 Widowed with two young children, thirty-four-year-old Ellen Jackson found herself in a desperate state. She moved into No. 10 Court, back of No. 84 Edward Street, Ladywood, with her widowed sister Hannah Stubbs but still struggled to make enough money as a dress maker and often told Hannah that she wished she and the children were out of this world. On this Sunday evening, Hannah went upstairs and was horrified to find nine-year-old Gertrude Amelia Jackson lying insensible on the landing. Entering Ellen's bedroom, she saw Ellen dying on the floor with seven-year-old Ernest Arthur Jackson shaking his mother and crying, 'Oh, mamma, don't you die.' Ernest told his aunt that Ellen had given them something nasty to drink from a teacup and so Hannah rushed the family round to a neighbouring chemist but Ellen died on the way. The two children were then taken to the General Hospital where they were diagnosed with strychnine poisoning but it was too late for Gertrude who died writhing in agony. Ernest recovered and the inquest returned a verdict of the wilful murder of Gertrude against Ellen who is then recorded to have committed suicide in a fit of temporary insanity.

28 NOVEMBER 1836 While she was shopping at the Market Hall with friends on the evening of 26 November, Mrs Andrews stopped at James Allcock's butcher's stall to enquire about the price of some meat. Allcock gave her a price but, thinking it too high for such a fatty piece, she declined and went to walk off. Allcock and his wife took instant umbrage and James refused to let Mrs Andrews leave the stall, dragging her back three times. When she attempted to struggle free, James struck her on the face, splitting her lip, while Mrs Allcock scratched her around the eye. Mrs Andrews reported the incident and, on this day, the butcher and his wife were brought before the police court on the charge of assault. James told the court that Mrs Andrews had been inebriated and insulted him, his wife and their meat, but when witnesses made it clear that Mrs Andrews was not drunk at all, the magistrates fined the Allcocks 20s each.

29 NOVEMBER 1875 Left alone at her home in Birchall Street on this Monday morning, ten-year-old Selina Beesley decided to remove a pot of boiling water from the fire. As she leaned over, her apron dangled into the fire and immediately ignited. Selina ran screaming into the yard, where several neighbours came to her assistance with wet cloths but she was extensively burned on the face and arms. A decision was made to convey Selina to the Queen's Hospital and at that moment her father, Joseph, came home. On seeing his daughter, he remarked, 'D__ her young blood; it serves her right.' Selina died of her injuries six days later and at the inquest the coroner returned a verdict of accidental death, remarking that Joseph was 'intolerably revolting' in his reaction to his only daughter's terrible injuries.

30 NOVEMBER 1856 As George Harvey was walking along Heath Street near his home this Sunday morning, three men suddenly came up, knocked him down and stamped on him violently. While George was lying stunned on the floor, one of the men – John Flynn – rifled through his pocket, stealing over 8s before they all ran away. Harvey gave chase, shouting for assistance, and a constable, hearing his cries, came across. Mr Harvey was giving a description his attackers when John Flynn appeared with a policeman and accused Harvey of attacking him. Luckily, witnesses verified Harvey's description of events and Flynn was arrested and charged with violent assault at Birmingham Police Court on 1 December. However, when the case was referred to Warwick's winter assizes, the evidence against Flynn was not considered strong enough and he was found not guilty.

DECEMBER

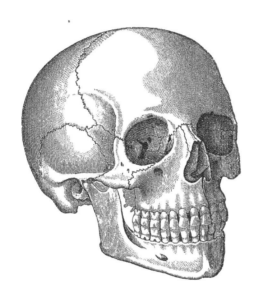

1 DECEMBER 1887 Readers of the *Birmingham Daily Post* would have been shocked to read on this day of the antics of sixty-four-year-old pauper Mary Clifford who resided at Birmingham Workhouse. In October 1887, she took to issuing violent threats to sixty-one-year-old Ann Boyle, another inmate of the workhouse, threating to murder her. On the morning of 29 November it seems that she decided to put her threats into action and, with a cry of 'You ___, I'll give it you now', Clifford threw herself at Boyle, hitting and pulling out lumps of her hair. Brought before the police court for assault, Clifford claimed that Boyle was making false accusations against her but Mr Bowen, clerk to the workhouse guardians, told the court that Clifford was a long-standing inmate who often assaulted others without the slightest reason and indeed there was a woman in the infirmary whose finger was deliberately cut off by the old woman. After hearing that scarcely a week passed without some kind of violence from Clifford, the court sentenced her to one month's imprisonment.

2 DECEMBER 1913 Twenty-eight-year-old fire-iron polisher Harry Smith had been married to his wife Ruth since 1907 but by 1914, the relationship had broken down to such an extent that Ruth left, taking their youngest child with her. By 2 December, Harry, finding out that Ruth was under the protection of Arthur Simmons at his house in Aston, went to see her and asked her to return. When she refused, he kissed their child and then turned to strike his wife. Arthur prevented Harry and they began to fight. The struggle spilled out into the yard and both men fell to the floor at which Harry drew a knife and stabbed Arthur in the shoulder, inflicting a wound 2in deep. Harry was arrested and tried at Birmingham Quarter Sessions in January 1914, charged with malicious wounding. Luckily for Harry, the wound caused no serious damage so the court returned a verdict of guilty of common assault and bound him over to be of good behaviour.

3 DECEMBER 1863 A fierce gale started at about six o'clock this Thursday and continued unabated for the rest of the day, causing damage to property around Birmingham, with the wind reaching violent proportions and several larger factory stacks in the city showing signs of imminent collapse. At midday, the chimney belonging to the Patent Enamel Company in Birchall Street suddenly toppled and crashed through Messrs Turner's fender, fire iron and screw warehouse. One of the rooms devastated by the falling stack contained a group of women wrapping screws. Sixteen-year-old Mary Maria Derry from Moseley Road was buried under the debris, her skull crushed in several places and her limbs fractured. The inquest found that the chimney was correctly constructed and Mary's death was therefore accidental.

4 DECEMBER 1862 The eight-month relationship between seventeen-year-old Alice Hinkley and twenty-year-old Henry Carter was regarded as happy and loving by family and friends. Brass founder Henry would often visit Alice at her home in Horton's Buildings, Bissell Street, where she lived with her family. On this Thursday, the couple spent a seemingly contented evening together before Henry got up to leave at half past ten and Alice followed him into the entry. A neighbour heard Henry say, 'Do you mean it?' and Alice reply, 'I do,' then there was the sudden sound of a gunshot and Henry was seen running away. Neighbours found Alice dying from a bullet wound in her back and, by the time she was conveyed home, she had already expired from blood loss caused by the bullet passing through her body and exiting through the neck. A hue and cry was raised for Henry but he returned within the hour, sobbing and begging to see Alice. He was immediately arrested and readily admitted to shooting his sweetheart. At his trial at Warwick Assizes in March 1863, Henry's defence argued that the gun went off accidentally and Henry had no intention to harm Alice, but he was found guilty of wilful murder and sentenced to death. He was executed on 6 April 1863 in front of Warwick Gaol, freely admitting that he had killed Alice after she tried to finish their relationship.

5 DECEMBER 1880 Irishman John Gately was employed as a labourer for a well-known horse breeder in Yardley and there were unfounded rumours that he was connected with the Irish Land League. On this Sunday afternoon, twenty-five-year-old Gately was in his lodgings in Solihull when an unidentified man went into the building, gained entry into Gately's room and shot him in the head at point-blank range, killing him instantly. Unbelievably the assassin escaped from the area and vanished without any witnesses coming forward. A book found in Gately's lodgings indicated his involvement with the Land League and a colleague testified to John's desire to leave the group. The murder seemed to be politically motivated but, despite numerous inquiries, no further evidence came to light and the murderer was never caught.

6 DECEMBER 1877 The Riley family of No. 2 Court, Newtown Row, were desperate for money, so when forty-two-year-old William sold a mattress from the house this Thursday evening, his wife Harriet followed him into the street and asked for the money to feed their five children who were 'clamming'. William refused her the money, instead punching her in the stomach before picking up a stone and throwing it at her. Birmingham Police Court were told that Mr Riley would not work, had not done so for several years, and that he had been in prison four times already for beating

his wife. When the stipendiary sentenced Riley to six months' hard labour for assault he replied, 'Thank you sir, I am very much obliged to you. They kept me the summer, and they'll have to keep me the winter.'

7 DECEMBER 1865 This day saw the death of fifty-six-year-old Ann Steadman who lived at No. 8 Bagnall's Buildings, Miller Street. On the evening of 5 December, Ann went into her husband Edward's workshop to put some coal on the fire and, as she did so, it is believed her foot caught against the leg of the bench and she fell, catching her head on the side of the furnace. Ann was knocked unconscious next to the stove and the heat scorched her clothing, which then caught fire. Edward found Ann aflame and, after extinguishing the flames, she was rushed to the General Hospital but her injuries proved fatal. The coroner held an inquest, which returned a verdict of accidental death.

8 DECEMBER 1868 A pool of water had accumulated in the newly dug foundation on waste ground between Wheeler Street and Russell Street in the days leading up to 8 December. At about half past nine this morning, three-year-old Joseph Day and his two-year-old cousin, Sarah Ann Thistlewood, left their homes in Russell Street to visit their grandmother who lived nearby. The two children were seen standing by the water with Joseph stamping the soil, when the earth gave way and the cousins were precipitated into the pool. Joseph and Sarah Ann were pulled from the water by passers-by but they had both drowned. The inquest returned a verdict of accidental death.

9 DECEMBER 1897 As cab driver Harold Field was travelling along Corporation Street near Aston Street, he was horrified to see an elderly gentleman step into the road directly in front of the cab. Despite shouting a warning and trying to halt, Field could not stop in time and seventy-seven-year-old tailor Daniel Hopkins walked head first into the horse, which knocked him beneath the cab. The wheels passed over Daniel's chest, crushing several ribs and puncturing a lung. Hopkins was taken to the General Hospital but he succumbed to his injuries five days later. At the inquest it was revealed that Hopkins was so bent with age that he had to walk with his head down and would never have seen the cab in time. The jury passed a verdict of accidental death.

10 DECEMBER 1892 When thirty-six-year-old Joseph Allsopp was admitted to Winson Green Asylum in December 1892, he was not deemed to be dangerous and was placed in a communal ward. On this Saturday night, Allsopp rose while

the other patients were asleep, picked up an earthenware jug and brained eighty-three-year-old Thomas Beasley. Allsopp then picked up the broken pieces and began attacking two other men in adjoining beds. Their screams attracted the attention of the attendants, who overpowered Allsopp. Thomas Beasley was already dead and one of the other patients, Thomas William Barnes, a fifty-nine-year-old bottle manufacturer, subsequently died in hospital. Allsopp was found guilty of wilful murder but, after expressing pleasure at their deaths, was removed to Broadmoor Criminal Lunatic Asylum where he died only eight months later from inflammation of the brain.

11 DECEMBER 1866 Thirty-one-year-old whip-stock maker Joseph Taylor began cohabitating with Elizabeth Desmond at No. 5 Court, Thorp Street, early in 1866 and the couple seemed happy, except when Taylor became drunk. On 13 October, Taylor came home intoxicated and started arguing with Elizabeth's father, fifty-five-year-old Dennis Desmond, until things got so heated that Dennis threw Taylor out of the house. However, Taylor later returned and Elizabeth let him in, thinking that her father was so drunk he was unlikely to wake. The couple were sleeping on a bed on the kitchen floor when, at about four o'clock the next morning, Dennis came downstairs and, seeing Joseph there, lost his temper, demanding, 'Have you got your bully in bed with you who threatened to take my life?' Joseph refused to leave and taunted Dennis, 'You old __, and I'll warm you for this,' whereupon Dennis threw a teapot at Joseph's head who retaliated by pushing Mr Desmond through a pane of glass. The fight escalated and Dennis picked up a knife, charging at Taylor. The two struggled for a moment before Taylor staggered backwards with a 2in wound on the left side of his abdomen through which pieces of intestines were protruding. Elizabeth took him to the General Hospital but Taylor died a few hours later from blood loss and intestine damage. Dennis was arrested and tried for manslaughter on 11 December 1866 at Warwick Assizes where he was found guilty but sentenced to only twelve months' imprisonment due to the provocation he received.

12 DECEMBER 1862 When seventy-eight-year-old retired agriculturist Richard Gibson was in the gentleman's retiring room at New Street Station this Friday evening, he heard the whistle for the departure of the seven o'clock Derby train. Rushing out on to the platform, Gibson tried to open one of the carriage doors even though the train was already moving. Just as he opened the door, Gibson lost his footing, pitching his body forward upon the footboards of the carriage with his legs still on the platform.

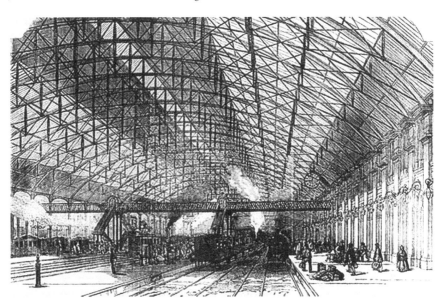

New Street Station, 1854. (Author's collection)

He was dragged along for several yards before disappearing under the wheels so that the rest of the carriages passed over him. Gibson was killed instantly, his neck dislocated and both arms almost severed from his dreadfully mangled body.

13   DECEMBER 1890 As Charlotte Palmer was passing along Staniforth Street this afternoon, she saw a group of young men engaged in a drunken quarrel. Despite not involving herself in the argument, one of the men, twenty-two-year-old Alfred Simpson of No. 24 Court, No. 5 House, Lower Tower Street, came up to Charlotte and knocked her down, kicking her in the back and stomach. Tried at Birmingham Police Court on 15 December, Alfred, who had been before the court seventeen times for various assaults, was sentenced to two months' hard labour for the attack on Charlotte. As he left the dock Simpson exclaimed, 'You're very good, gentlemen; I expected six months.'

14   DECEMBER 1865 On this day an inquest was held on the death of a baby boy, the infant child of Martha Yateman. On 5 December, Martha, a twenty-four-year-old laundress lodging in the house of Mrs Poyntney in No. 11 Court, William Street, Ladywood, left for work. Shortly afterwards one of Mrs Poyntney's children ran into the courtyard where labourer George Jones was standing and told him something was burning on the fire in the kitchen. Jones entered the house and was shocked to see the naked body of a newly born child in the fire. There was a horrid stench of burning flesh and, when George

removed the body, he found the head and neck burnt away. The police were called and Martha Yateman, when apprehended, readily admitted to the child being hers. Martha told the authorities that she had delivered the child the night before but he had been stillborn so, before leaving for work, she had placed the body on the fire. Due to the burn damage, the post-mortem examination could not determine if the baby had lived or not so the coroner remarked that the only verdict the jury could return was 'found dead on a fire'.

15 DECEMBER 1897 It was fifty-four-year-old Abraham Normansell's birthday on this day and he was at work at the Corporation Gasworks, Saltley Road. The married father of seven from Denbigh Street was engaged with his assistant Kelsey in moving coal from one floor to the next by means of a lift. The lift hole was protected by a block, which was removed to allow the wagons to pass but should, according to the rules of the works, have been replaced immediately after the trucks were in the cage. On this Wednesday afternoon, Kelsey went down the lift with a loaded wagon without replacing the block; Abraham, expecting to find the lift in the up position, pushed his truck into the hole and fell with it. Kelsey was injured by the falling wagon but Abraham was killed instantly by the 20ft drop. At the inquest, Kelsey stated that the stop block was never used but the gas company denied this. A verdict of accidental death was returned, but the jury suggested an automatic stop block should be fitted.

16 DECEMBER 1891 When sixty-two-year-old iron stamper Jeremiah Pettit of Tillingham Street, Sparkbrook, lost his job in 1890, he made several attempts to gain employment, even going to America with one of his sons to find work. He returned depressed and unable to sleep, complaining of pains in the head. After several months, Mr Pettit found a job but the strangeness of manner did not abate and he would tell his wife Louisa that he wished they could die together. By December 1891, Jeremiah had fallen into the habit of walking around their bedroom for most of the night. Early on this Wednesday morning, Louisa was woken by Jeremiah who was attempting to stab her in the stomach; she sprang out of bed and rushed next door for help. Neighbours eventually entered the Pettits bedroom and found Jeremiah dead on the floor, four stab wounds in his chest made by a penknife nearby. The post-mortem at the inquest revealed that, although the heart was punctuated, death would have been slow and painful. The inquest jury returned a verdict of *felo de se* following upon insanity on the father of seven.

17 DECEMBER 1867 Inside the yard of Mr Samuel Walker's brass foundry and rolling mills in Fazeley Street, was a well about 100ft deep which furnished the necessary water supply for the engine. The well needed regular cleaning and,

on 16 December at about six o'clock in the evening, sixty-four-year-old engineer Joseph Dainty decided to inspect it, taking off his jacket before descending. The foreman became aware that Dainty had not reappeared and, after getting no response from the well, sent down forty-five-year-old father-of-six James Farrow who remerged somewhat stupefied, saying that there was no sign of Dainty but the air was 'foul'. Against advice, Farrow descended again but there was a sudden splash and he too could not be reached. By now several men were assembled around the well and millwright Henry Jones (a married man with three young children) volunteered to enter the well with a rope tied around him. Unfortunately it is believed that Jones untied the rope when he found Farrow and, also losing consciousness, could not be pulled back up. Any further attempts were prevented and instead the well was pumped and a fan placed to ventilate the air. Finally, early this morning, the bodies of the three men were recovered, all suffocated by carbonic acid gas. On hearing of her father's death, twenty-year-old Catherine Dainty collapsed and died within days.

18 DECEMBER 1889 On this day, fifty-eight-year-old Charles Lester Higginbottom was tried for the wilful murder of his seventy-eight-year-old landlady Winifred Phillips at her home in Guildford Street. Higginbottom had been lodging with the Phillips family for several years when, on 13 July 1889, he and Winfred quarrelled and Charles was asked to leave the house at the end of the week, which he agreed to do. On 18 July, Higginbottom went to work as usual but returned for dinner sometime before one o'clock. Witnesses later testified that Higginbottom's conduct seemed perfectly normal and no argument was heard from the house. However, at about six o'clock, a neighbour entered the sitting room to find Mrs Phillips leaning back on the couch, frothing at the mouth and with blood running from a large head wound. The neighbour ran into the passage where, confronted by Higginbottom brandishing a knife and threating to do her in, she made it to the door and rushed for help. Mrs Phillips was taken to the hospital while PC Stanley searched the house, where he found a coal hammer covered in blood and hair before stumbling on Higginbottom in an upstairs bedroom holding a large carving knife and with his throat cut from ear to ear. Mrs Phillips died later that night but Higginbottom eventually recovered from his horrific injuries and was tried at Warwick Assizes. He showed no remorse for his crime and instead expressed regret that he 'did not do for the lot because they nagged him so'. There was no evidence of insanity so Higginbottom was found guilty and sentence to death. He was executed at Warwick Gaol on 7 January 1890 and, when the hanging took place, his neck wound split open with blood pouring 'in torrents' over the ground.

19 DECEMBER 1836 William Owen had spent the evening at his local public house before making his way home towards Hockley Hill. As he reached The Old Tree public house, Great Hampton Street, Owen met three men and, as the road was narrow and he was intoxicated, bumped into them. One of the men, Thomas Maslin, took exception to Owen's drunken progress and pushed him to the ground but Owen retaliated, charging at Maslin in an attempt to fight. Owen was no match for the young man who was holding a tasselled stick which he used to strike Owen, knocking him to the floor several times. Owen staggered to his feet but he was clearly distressed and frothing at the mouth. As Maslin and his companions walked away, witnesses rushed to Owen but he collapsed and died. The watch were called, who arrested Maslin in Newhall Street, but the post-mortem could find no probable cause of death so the inquest returned a verdict of death by visitation of God and Maslin walked free from court.

20 DECEMBER 1857 After an argument between the Miller and Brough families living in Barr Street, Susan Miller decided to continue the disagreement by visiting the Brough home this evening with labourer friend Owen Keepe. Miller and Keepe battered down the door with a poker before attacking Mary Brough with a metal box lid. As Mary lay on the floor almost senseless with a serious head injury, Keepe dragged her by the hair into an adjoining entry where he brutally kicked her in various part of the body. The couple then proceeded to smash up the Brough's house with stones and bricks until the police arrived to arrest them. Susan Miller and Owen Keepe were brought before Birmingham Police Court charged with violent assault. Although they were found guilty and ordered to pay a fine of 20s, Miller and Keepe showed no remorse, leaving the dock vowing that they would never pay a penny.

21 DECEMBER 1883 John Chaplain from Gladstone Place, Lees Street, Lodge Road, was employed by the goods department of the Great Western Railway at Hockley. On the evening of 21 December, the seventeen-year-old was shunting some trucks when one of them caught him on the back and knocked him down. One of the truck wheels passed over Chaplain's left leg, crushing it severely below the knee. It was clear that the leg was badly damaged as blood was flowing freely from the wound but for the next hour the only assistance given was a handkerchief laid across the leg; Chaplain lay on the rails until finally a trolley was obtained and he was taken to the General Hospital. He died soon after from blood loss and shock. The doctor at the inquest stated that had assistance been given sooner then Chaplain would likely have survived.

22 DECEMBER 1879 A shocking discovery was made on this day at Hamstead Colliery when ganger John Michaels entered the workman's hut nearby. The cabin contained a fireplace with a chimney at least 10ft deep and 15in wide, and from the opening Michaels could see skeletal feet dangling, attached to a body charred to a cinder. It was found to be the remains of twenty-one-year-old George Watkins who was last seen the night before when he was turned away from his lodging because of drunken behaviour. Watkins, it was presumed, went to the cabin and, finding it locked, had attempted to climb down the chimney where he became trapped. Unfortunately a large fire would have been left burning in the fireplace and Watkins slowly roasted to death.

23 DECEMBER 1893 A great deal of animosity had built up between the 'Park Street Gang' and the 'Barford Street Gang' and there were regular fights between the two. The Park Street Gang was in the habit of meeting at the Museum Concert Hall, Digbeth, and, after an argument between rival members, the 'Barford Streets' decided to go to the concert hall to confront them. On this Saturday evening, several members of the gangs started to fight outside the museum vaults, using their buckled belts to attack each other. At some point, eighteen-year-old nail maker John Thomas Cherry of the Barford Streets drew a knife, walked up to rival gang member twenty-year-old John Metcalf and stabbed him in the neck just below the ear. Metcalf staggered across the road and died outside a shop. The gangs fled but Cherry admitted to several people that he was the man who had 'chivied' Metcalf, not expecting the wound to be fatal. When he was arrested five days later, Cherry denied any involvement but witnesses had seen him with the knife and he was sent to Birmingham Assizes in March 1894, charged with wilful murder. The jury returned a verdict of manslaughter and Cherry was sentenced to five years' penal servitude. Cherry, on hearing the sentence, smiled, waved and laughed up to the gallery before tripping gaily from the dock.

24 DECEMBER 1892 Shooting gallery owner Eliza Wilson set up her stall at a fair located in Hurst Street on some vacant land just below Day's Concert Hall. Wilson employed eighteen-year-old Daniel James Burke and, on this Saturday night, she asked him to light up the boxes at the end of the enclosed range. Burke was walking behind the metal screen when a boy noticed him fall to the floor with blood flowing copiously from a head wound. Taken to the Queen's Hospital, it was clear that Burke had died instantly when a bullet had entered his right temple. The next day, the screen was examined and found to consist of several pieces of sheet iron, riveted together. In one of the sheets was a hole, which was directly in line with where Burke fell.

At the inquest it was suggested that the holes were already in the metal and, by a particularly unfortunate circumstance, a bullet had gone through just as Burke was passing; the jury returned a verdict of misadventure.

25 DECEMBER 1860 In November 1860, thirty-three-year-old Hephzibah Sumner left her husband, thirty-nine-year-old Charles Sumner, due to his ill treatment and moved in with one of her sisters in Prospect Row. On Christmas night, Charles sent a message to the heavily pregnant Hephzibah, asking to meet at the Bell Inn, Prospect Row. When she got there, Charles told Hephzibah that she had to return to their home in Harding Street. She refused and Charles took her by the neck and began striking her around the chest and face with his fist. Terrified, Hephzibah told him she would go with him but her husband was having none of it, 'No you won't; I have come for it and mean to do it tonight.' With that he dragged her to the liquor vaults and beat her till she lost consciousness. Several customers tried to pull Charles away but it wasn't until one of them hit him over the head with a stick that he was prevented from doing further damage. A doctor was called and it was expected that Hephzibah would die of her injuries, but she was well enough to give evidence against her husband in January 1861 where she told the court that she had feared for her life. The Bench sentenced Charles to six months' imprisonment, expressing their sorrow that they could not inflict a heavier sentence.

26 DECEMBER 1836 On this day, Joseph Bisseker of Aston was brought before magistrates charged with assault and attempted rape. On 21 December, Bisseker, a married man, met seventeen-year-old Ann Smith in town and persuaded her to accompany him for the afternoon. Rather naively, Smith left her female companion and went with Joseph to various public houses but drank very little. However, when Bisseker tried to get Smith into a house of ill fame in Little Colmore Street that night, she rushed from the house and sought protection in the dwelling of a Mrs Cowell in Colmore Street. Bisseker followed and, rendered desperate by drink and disappointed passion, commenced a violent assault on Smith, threw furniture and threatened Mrs Cowell and her son with a knife. With difficulty Bisseker was arrested and at Birmingham Police Court he was fined over £10 and bound over to keep the peace.

27 DECEMBER 1884 In 1866, after over seventeen years of marriage, screw tool-maker Henry Kimberley left his wife to set up home in Pershore Street, Birmingham, with Harriet Stewart. The couple, who lived together as man and wife under the surname Stevens, initially seemed very happy but, by December 1884, Harriet decided

James Berry, executioner.
(Courtesy of the Black Country Museum)

to leave Henry due his cruel treatment of her daughter from a previous relationship. Fifty-three-year-old Henry agreed to a separation and moved out of the house on 18 December but within a few days he was begging to return. On this Saturday morning, Henry again approached thirty-nine-year-old Harriet but, when she refused to take him back, he threated to have his revenge. By seven o'clock in the evening, Harriet was sitting in the snug of the White Hart Inn in Paradise Street, drinking with thirty-five-year old landlady Emma Palmer, when Henry entered and began arguing with the two women. Harriet repeated her determination to maintain the separation, whereupon Henry pulled out a five-chamber revolver and fired at both women. Harriet was shot in the skull while a bullet entered Mrs Palmer's neck and travelled into her chest. Customers immediately overpowered Henry and the two women were rushed to the Queen's Hospital. Henry was charged with attempted murder but, when Emma Palmer died of her injuries two weeks later, he was committed to Birmingham Assizes for wilful murder. On 26 February 1885, Henry was found guilty of Emma's murder and sentenced to death. Despite appeals for a reprieve, Henry was executed at Winson Green Prison on 17 March by James Berry. Harriet Stewart made a full recovery.

28 DECEMBER 1889 Although twenty-year-old Kate Wright had only worked in the offices at Buller, Bickley and Cross Manufactory in Great Charles Street for ten days, she had already proved to be a conscientious and enthusiastic employee. On 17 December 1889, Wright was working on some invoices and there were several that she could not make out. Hearing the 'young master' was about to leave the premises, she quickly left the room to follow him, not realising that a trap door to the cellar was open just by the office. Wright fell nearly 10ft to the floor below where she was found unconscious and taken to her home in Arthur Street, Small Heath. Initially, Wright just seemed shaken but she had fractured the base of her skull and died on this day from paralysis of the brain. The coroner returned a verdict of accidental death but recommended the trap door be made safer; Mr Buller said he would do so and would be compensating Wright's parents for their sad loss.

29 DECEMBER 1858 On the evening of 28 December 1858, ten-year-old Mary Ann Adderley and her eleven-year-old friend Ellen Brooks were found destitute in Summer Row. Brought before Birmingham Police Court on this day, Inspector Norton explained that the two girls were frequent inmates of the workhouse. It seems that Adderley and Brooks were found wandering the streets by a policeman who had taken them to the workhouse. However, Mr Edmonds, the workhouse porter, refused admission as it was after nine o'clock so the girls were turned away. The defence council remarked that 'one of the consequences [was] that they were tempted to street-walking and its consequent evils'. The judge strongly suggested the rule needed to be addressed before advising Adderley and Brooks to go to their friends.

30 DECEMBER 1894 Wealthy inhabitants of Wylde Green would traditionally distribute soup during the New Year period and Mrs Page of the Wylde Green Hotel was no exception. Anyone who called at the hotel on the night of 29 December was given a warming bowl of the beef and pearl broth, which they gladly accepted. However, by early this morning, all the people who had taken some soup began suffering from terrible stomach cramps, vomiting and diarrhoea. Nearly 100 people were struck down but forty-seven-year-old Esther Ivens was particularly ill and died on 8 January 1895. The subsequent inquest brought forward several possible causes for the poisonings, including deliberate use of arsenic or incorrect use of brine by the butcher, but a chemical examination of the soup revealed that it contained bacteria from sewage, which was believed to have come from an open drain in the kitchen where the soup was prepared. Mrs Ivens' death was judged as accidental poisoning and no blame was attributed to Mrs Page or the butcher who supplied the beef.

31 DECEMBER 1888 Minnie Louisa Foster left her house in Balsall Heath on the evening of Saturday, 29 December to teach French lessons in Moseley. As she crossed the street in Hertford Road, Balsall Heath, a milk float, believed to be driven by twenty-two-year-old George Quiney, suddenly appeared and hit Foster, knocking her to the ground. Quiney made no attempt to stop but whipped his horse on and drove swiftly away. Foster was picked up but was found to be dead. The accident had been seen by several witnesses who recognised Quiney and he was arrested and charged on this day with causing death by dangerous driving. A large number of witnesses were called but the jury returned a verdict of accidental death. The jury also expressed an opinion that Quiney, who still denied any involvement, was the driver and deserved severe censure for his heartless conduct in not staying to render assistance.

ABOUT THE AUTHOR

KAREN EVANS is a primary school teacher with a love of history. After tracing her family tree for over twenty years, she stumbled upon a murderer in its branches and quickly became fascinated with the macabre elements of genealogy, going on to write articles for history magazines such as *Family Tree*. She has previously published *A Grim Almanac of Staffordshire* for The History Press.

BIBLIOGRAPHY

Newspapers

Aris's Birmingham Gazette
Birmingham Daily Gazette
Birmingham Daily Mail
Birmingham Daily Post
Express and Star
Birmingham Gazette

Birmingham Journal
Illustrated Police News
Staffordshire Advertiser
Coventry Herald
Coventry Standard
Lloyd's Weekly Newspaper

Websites

www.billdargue.jimdo.com/glossary-brief-histories/a-brief-history-of-birmingham/
    victorian-birmingham
www.birminghamhistory.co.uk/forum
www.blackcountrymuse.com
www.libraryofbirmingham.com/lostpubs

Lightning Source UK Ltd.
Milton Keynes UK
UKOW06f0328150916

283031UK00001B/12/P